CW00658950

To all at Warren Clase,
nerve centre of
Floodlit Dreams . . .

A *Dazzling* DARKNESS

Best wishes,

Ian R.

A *Dazzling* DARKNESS

THE DARREN BARKER STORY
with Ian Ridley

Published by Floodlit Dreams Ltd
www.floodlitdreams.com

Published by Floodlit Dreams Ltd, 2015.

Copyright © Darren Barker and Ian Ridley, 2015.

Darren Barker and Ian Ridley have asserted their rights under the Copyright, Design and Patents Act of 1988 to be identified as the authors of this work.

All rights reserved. No part of this publication may be reproduced, stored in a retrieval system or transmitted in any form or by any means electronic, mechanical, photocopying, recording or otherwise, without the prior permission of both the copyright owner and the above publisher of this book.

A CIP catalogue record for this book is available from the British Library.

ISBN 978-0-9926585-3-3

Floodlit Dreams Ltd
5-6 George St
St Albans
Herts AL3 4ER

www.floodlitdreams.com

Cover pictures by Alex Ridley
Cover designed by Mike McMonagle and Gemma Kao
Typeset by Peloton Publishing

For you, Gal. We did it.

A DAZZLING DARKNESS

CONTENTS

A DAZZLING DARKNESS

CONTENTS

INTRODUCTION
BY IAN RIDLEY

My name is Ian and I am a recovering alcoholic. It means that I am damaged – and fascinated by damaged people. It can make life difficult, dangerous even – but interesting. It can also be useful if you are a writer, though God knows I fought against being one. Still do.

A few years after quitting drinking, more than 25 years ago now, I hit some kind of wall. The relief at the end of the madness, sadness and badness had given way to the mundane realities of daily life. Responsibilities and feelings grew overwhelming. The pain of years of learned, self-defeating behaviour kicked in.

On the surface all was well. I had a good job as a sports writer – lovely family, nice house, good car. But as the title of a book by Bob Earll, guru to many recovering from addictive illness had it: I got tired of pretending. Pretending all was well and that I was too.

I had just written my first book and vowed I would never write another – like a drunk swearing abstinence after a bender that had produced fearsome sweats and terrors. The experience of writing at length and in detail, the discipline and dredging of personal resources, had drained and soured me.

I had been tested to my limits physically, emotionally and mentally and was not about to go through all that again. I had put something of myself into the book and did not enjoy it being in the public domain where people would know something about me now. I was just a journalist. Just a sports journalist. I chronicled other people's lives in just enough depth – the inadequate but manageable depth that newspaper space allowed.

Giving up writing books was going to be easy, I thought. It was certainly the simplest way of avoiding the fear of the blank page. Except the nagging feeling that this was what I might be supposed to do with my life, and my sobriety, would not go away. I was torn, between the comfortable life – stressful at times but comfortable enough thanks to training and experience – of the short-order sports writer's words and the depth and duty of the author's calling.

A friend by the name of Jimmy Mulville suggested I go see a man. His name was Bruce Lloyd and he saved my career – and probably my life.

Bruce operated from a house in South London, next to The Oval cricket ground. People from all walks of life, high and low, famous musicians and actors, moneyed business people, would be seen between reduced-rate clients who could barely afford it. They all came and went quietly, anonymously, because they could get what he offered nowhere else.

Bruce was, is, an intuitively brilliant therapist. A recovering alcoholic himself, his particular style of therapy is not easy to define. Put simply, he takes damaged people, encourages them to acknowledge and own the pain of their trauma, and teaches them how to manage the damage. Working in a bubble of a consulting room from which he rarely ventures out socially, he sets them on the path they are meant to be taking in life and supports and validates them every step of the way.

Me? He got me writing books again. It meant I did what I think I was supposed to do in my recovery from alcoholism: write *Addicted*, the story of Tony Adams and the Arsenal and England captain's recovery from his own alcoholism, which helped many people. It meant also that I got to write in *Floodlit Dreams* about my time as a chairman of my home town football club and chronicle soothingly my grief at the death of my father during that period.

Then, seven years ago, Bruce said he wanted to introduce me to someone he was also working with. He had their permission, he said. They were not only willing, but actually keen to meet me. The lad was a boxer, name of Darren Barker, the Commonwealth champion, but something was blocking him from stepping up to higher levels, was troubling him so much, indeed, that he was threatening to quit every month or two.

And so one cold February Friday night back in 2008 I found myself with Bruce at a boxing venue in East London, sitting between him and a burly man, big too of personality, by the name of Bryn Robertson. Like Jimmy Mulville with me, Bryn had been the one to point Darren towards Bruce. I would meet, too, Darren's trainer Tony Sims. Both men, it would transpire, would have stories of their own that suddenly made sense of my own role in all this.

A couple of weeks after the fight, I turned up at Bruce's house to meet Darren properly. Nervously, Bruce introduced us. This was uncomfortable for him. He was not in the habit of putting his clients together, of breaking cover. He thrived on his own privacy and preferred to keep us all separate, all special as individuals.

Bruce just had a feeling that Darren and I would connect, that he had a story that was begging to be told – deserved to be because it might resonate with many – and that I might be the one to tell it. Bruce's own nervousness was worth a greater good, he reasoned.

Darren and I did indeed hit it off. I was taken by his understated strength, his quiet dignity, as I listened that day to his poignant, gripping back story of family tragedy. He had good reason to want his story out there, for both his own catharsis of disclosure and the help it might offer to others.

What follows is Darren's vivid, poignant first-hand story. I have sought to capture in all its detail the plumbing of depths and scaling of heights. It is a story that would travel from the earthy, claustrophobic East End boxing cockpit of York Hall to the glitz and glamour of world title fights in Atlantic City in the United States. Taking in, on the way, lonely gyms and an even lonelier therapist's consulting room.

It embraces the ruthless, physical toll that boxing can extract, the agonies of a training camp and the ferocity on the night that television can dilute. The screen, even in high definition and super slow motion, just cannot reveal properly the viciousness of the blows as when seen from ringside – with the gloves nowhere near as cushioned as might be expected. Nor can it capture the sweat that glistens in the arc lights. Even the modern sharpness of cameras struggles with the scarlet hue of the blood that seeps from cuts and nostrils, the black that surrounds eyes, the red-rawness of the weals that stripe rib cage and back.

And no visual medium can convey like words the private mental struggle involved in getting into a ring, a struggle that was always more acute for Darren given the complexity and contradictions of a man who would have to endure the blackest of darknesses to get to a place where he could dazzle in a boxing ring.

Darren's story also takes in the gripping tales of Tony Sims, Bryn Robertson and Bruce Lloyd, whose own vivid personal experiences, I would discover, mirrored Darren in so many ways. Their stories are told in chapters of their own, at what I hope are appropriate and relevant points in the narrative. I introduce them and their back stories, then let them speak for themselves.

This special set of people and the circumstances they shared - I believe it to have been spiritual ordination rather than merely coincidence that brought them together – would conspire to help heal a man in emotional agonies and soothe their own souls. I would learn that hard men hurt too.

I would also meet men who smoothed his journey, such as the promoter Eddie Hearn and someone more than a sponsor in

Luke Chandler. All of them would have their own contributions to the story that were telling and worth telling.

Boxing's smoky heyday may have gone, terrestrial TV its mostly departed, barely interested outlet, and now has only the smaller audiences of satellite television to comfort and finance it. Its art and science may struggle to compete with the crass, vogue violence and showbiz of cage fighting and wrestling. But it still has great men and great nights that retain the capacity to fire the imagination. Through hard times and fight nights, Darren Barker embodied the heroism it retains.

In the unpromising location of a small boxing hall in Bethnal Green followed by the consulting room of a London therapist, came the start of a deeply spiritual story that I came to see I was supposed to write because of my own damage and struggle to fulfill my calling. I realised that it was damage gifted to me so I could understand that of such as Darren Barker and be the channel to bring it to kindred suffering souls whose own losses and pain might be eased by empathy. And to those who might delight in the redemption of the human spirit.

Not that I knew any of that on that first fight night, nor that this would take seven years. I was just going to watch a boxer take some early steps back on his chosen, intended path after a few wrong turnings when touched and tortured by grief.

I had no idea then that Darren's path would take him over broken glass and burning coals onwards, ultimately, to a glittering prize. But it did, gloriously, and this is how it happened.

St Albans, August 2015

NO
GUTS
NO
GLORY
MANOR PLACE BATHS
MONDAY, 4TH APRIL, 1977
A TEAM MATCH
One of Europe's Leading Boxing Clubs
Non-Diners £3.00
NO UNAUTHORISED PERSON
BEYOND THIS POINT UNLESS
CRB REGISTERED.
Fire
exit

I

THE FABULOUS BARKER BOYS

Through these fields of destruction,
Baptisms of fire,
I've witnessed your suffering,
As the battle raged higher.
And though they did hurt me so bad,
In the fear and alarm,
You did not desert me,
My brothers in arms.

Brothers In Arms
Dire Straits

1

DEATH AT DAWN

Now I knew for sure it was bad. It was 8am on a Sunday morning in early December and cars were at a standstill on the M1 where it meets the M25, still 10 miles from the hospital. It's got to be serious if the motorway's not moving and they're backed up that far when it's early morning on a weekend. And going north, rather than towards the city.

I was in a total panic as I drove up from my Nan Janet and Grandad Rodney's home in Barnet, North London, where I was living, and just kept thinking what a mad, beautiful kid my brother was. I had tried to talk him out of going but Gary was his own man, even at the age of just 19. He was stubborn and determined. It was part of his charm and part of what made him a great boxing talent and a smashing brother.

We'd had a lovely night out on the Saturday. Both of us had won our fights the previous evening, me my 14th as a professional against Paul Samuels at Goresbrook Leisure Centre in Dagenham and Gary as an amateur for Repton, the East London club where we had both learned our trade, up in Scotland against the Gilmerton club of Edinburgh. He had flown down during the day and we met up at a dinner show organised by my trainer, Tony Sims, at the Prince Regent Hotel out at Chigwell in Essex.

After that, alive, alert and not ready for sleep, we fancied a night out up in the West End. So we went home, got changed and ended up in a club called Strawberry Moons, just off Regent

Street. There were five of us, including our other brother Lee, the middle one, and a couple of mates in Nicky and Ben, all in the mood for some fun.

It was buzzy and noisy in the club but it was funny how Gary and I found ourselves in a quiet corner and talked like we hadn't done for a while. About life a bit. About boxing and women a lot. He was the natural boxer, technical and outrageously gifted, and had won the Amateur Boxing Association national schools title within a year of taking up the sport. He had even gone to America and won a Junior Olympic Games gold medal. Everyone felt sure he would go on to represent Great Britain in the Beijing Olympics in 2008. He was already on lottery money through Sport England. I was the one who had to work hard to hit the heights.

I had a beer or two. Gary was lively enough without one. Full of beans, as usual. We got a night bus home at about 3am, still just enjoying ourselves and our own company until a couple of loud, boisterous lads got on and started throwing their weight around. One of them pushed Gary and refused to apologise. They both got chinned. I still have a scar on a knuckle on my right hand from a tooth mark to remind me of December 10th, 2006. Not that I would ever have forgotten that date anyway.

We got off the bus at High Barnet and walked down through the freezing cold, quiet streets surrounding the old Barnet football ground at Underhill to Mum and Dad's, where I left him to go round the corner to Grandad's. I was living there these days, with our family three-bedroom home having got too small to hold us all now we were all grown up. Lee and Gary were sharing a room and sister Daisy was in the box room.

Gary said he fancied driving up to see his girlfriend Jessica in Leicester, where she was at University, while the roads were quiet. Said he would be all right after a cup of coffee. I told him not to be so stupid. Told him to have a kip for a few hours and then set out. It would still be quiet on a Sunday morning and the roads would be less icy. He was a proper heavy sleeper and I thought that if he got his head down, he would wake up and be fine. He agreed. Told me to get off to bed.

And so I did. What I didn't know was that Gary would wake Mum up at 5.30am to tell her he was going to Leicester and she would try but fail to talk him out of it. And so she boiled a kettle for hot water to de-ice the windscreen and told him to drive safely. A little while later she would get hold of him on his phone while he was filling up with petrol at South Mimms service station to tell him that if he got tired, he should pull off the motorway and rest. She also told him she loved him.

I was woken up around 9.30am by Grandad banging on my bedroom door. "Wake up. Gal has had an accident," he was shouting. He was in a right state. The police had apparently been round to Mum and Dad's to say something had happened to him and to take them to the Luton and Dunstable hospital. They had rung Grandad before setting off.

Disorientated, bleary-eyed, I threw on a tracksuit and the two of us jumped into my Mercedes coupe, stopping quickly for petrol on the way. My head was clearing now and I felt sure Grandad was getting too panicky. He and the whole family were worriers by nature. This was Gary. He would be all right. It couldn't be serious.

Now, 10 miles south of the hospital, I knew it was. People were out of their cars, talking to each other, the way they do when they have been in a motorway queue for a while. I wasn't having any of that. I flew up the hard shoulder, ignoring the dirty looks. One lorry driver pulled over to stop me when he saw me coming in his mirror. I gave him plenty of aggro, told him my brother had been involved in an accident and he backed off and let me through.

I parked right in front of the entrance to the hospital and dashed in, telling the reception who I was. Or whose brother I was. They directed me to a small room where Mum and Dad were sitting, both of them crying. I will never forget the first thing Dad said to me: "He's not with us any more, Dal."

Grandad let out a loud scream. Daisy was there and screaming too. Lee and his girlfriend Enza would soon arrive. I went into shock. Said nothing. Nothing ever prepares you for a moment like that. How can it? Being told by your Dad that your brother is not with you any more? That he is dead.

Dad said Gary was in the next room and I should go and see him, that I should go and say goodbye. I'd be glad I did one day, he said. But that was the last thing I wanted. I wanted to remember him as the smiling kid full of life in a London club.

I walked out into the corridor and could see the door to the next room open just a little bit. As I wandered past, my head spinning with what had happened and wondering where we all went next as a family and how we would ever recover from this, I caught a glimpse of Gary laid out on a trolley. A rage came over me. I went mental. I ran down the corridor and put my fist into a door. It was already smarting from the tooth mark of a few hours earlier on the night bus. Now it hurt like hell.

Having snatched a look at him, and calming down as sadness began to replace the anger, I decided that I might as well go in and see Gary. Dad was right. In years to come, I would be glad I did.

I walked tentatively through the door and stood by the trolley. Later, there was a news report that he had "a large number of wounds" as a result of his little silver hire-purchase Ford Fiesta hitting the central crash barrier and rolling just south of Toddington services at 6am but he didn't look banged up right now. Mind you, all I could see was his head and face, which had just little cuts visible. From the neck down, he was covered by a sheet. Later, we would be told that the cause of death was "internal injuries."

I just stared at him. You mad, beautiful kid.

What do you do, what you say when you see someone you love just lying there and not responding? My fist was still hurting but the physical pain was nothing compared to this emotional ache. I cried. I sat there. I talked to him the way I would also do later during my prayers. Don't know for how long. For as long as I could bear to look at his face one last time. I was so torn between going and staying. I didn't want to leave and never see him again but I didn't want to stay and see him like this.

When I could take the pain no longer, I left and that was it. A young life over just like that. I went back to the waiting room where the family was still sitting, now quieter. Shock had set in. Mum went into Mum mode, looking after us all and worrying about us.

The police who had brought Mum and Dad up to the hospital had left by now so the two of them came back with me and Grandad in my car. Nobody said much on the 45-minute journey. They just cried in the back. Nothing much needed to be said. We all knew it had changed our lives forever. As I drove south, cars going north were still backed up. The wreckage of Gary's car may have been cleared but the traffic was still a mess. I was the only driver on the road who knew what the problem was. The journey was a blur. I was on auto-pilot.

Once home, I switched on my mobile, having turned it off when I lay down to sleep after persuading Gary, or so I thought, not to drive to Leicester. It was backed up with messages and texts. I couldn't face them. Then it rang and I picked up when I saw the name of my trainer Tony Sims come up. He was in bits and couldn't believe it. "Tell me it ain't true, Daz," he kept saying. But it was.

There was one person I felt I ought to ring, my girlfriend Gemma who deserved to know and who was still living then with her Mum and Dad, Janet and Charlie, in Southgate. I hated having to tell her.

Later, when I did finally check my messages, there would be one from Gary.

'Feel fine,' it said. 'Going to drive up there. Tell Mum and Dad not to worry.' It had been sent at just after 5am. I stared at it in disbelief.

I thought about what a great boxer he was but, more importantly, what a great kid he was too and I wept. For him. For me. He was my boxing soul mate. Boxing? Couldn't think about doing that again. Had no interest in it. I just kept thinking about how weird and empty the future was going to be without Gary. How was I ever going to fight again? I couldn't even contemplate getting in a ring.

The only solace to be had was in that intimate conversation we had had hours before he died, as if it was meant to be. That and all the wonderful times we had had together as amateurs coming up through the Repton ranks, me, four years older, always looking out for my brother in arms.

2

THE OPENING PUNCHES

Boxing was always in the background when I was growing up, what with my Dad Terry having been an amateur champion, but it was never pushed down our throats. He rarely brought the subject up, though always answered questions we asked him and told us all the great stories. Like how there came to be an England vest hanging up in the house and trophies all around the place, from London Amateur Boxing Association winner to national champion, representing Repton, which was not too far from where he grew up in Haringey.

It was in 1980, at light flyweight and aged just 18, that Dad won the ABA title at Wembley Arena and registered the amazing achievement of winning junior and senior national championships in the same season. It can't be done any more. Boxers are not allowed to fight as juniors and seniors simultaneously. That night, he beat the great John Lyon, who would go on to win eight ABA titles, fight twice for Great Britain at Olympic Games, win a Commonwealth gold medal for England and be awarded the MBE. But my Dad beat him. And the winner of the heavyweight title that night was a bloke by the name of Frank Bruno.

Around the time I was born – on May 19th, 1982, and named Darren Francis Barker – Dad took a year out but came back for a while to have another 10 fights before calling it a day at the age of 24. I suppose, then, boxing must have been in me. You can fight many things and many people but you can't fight nature.

Dad and my Mum Jacqueline met – Terry meets Jacqui: sounds like that old Kinks' song Waterloo Sunset - after Dad's family had moved out to Edgware at the end of the Northern Line, Mum being from nearby Harrow, where I was born, at Northwick Park hospital. They married young, at the age of 21, and moved to Barnet when I was 10 months old.

Lee came next, on February 27th, 1984 and Gary arrived in 1987, on February 2nd. Our sister Daisy made up the quartet of kids, born on November 29th, 1990. She got the box room where I, as the eldest, had been privileged to bed down, and I then shared a room with Lee and Gary. Somehow we squeezed three beds in, two of them bunk beds and we would all swap around regularly. It was part of the fun.

Dad provided for us all, first as a hod carrier then as a painter and decorator, and instilled one important instruction in us: always look out for each other. With Grandad Rodney and Nan Janet from Dad's side of the family living near our house in Mays Lane, we were literally a close family.

We all went to Underhill primary school, near the Barnet football ground, though I would grow up a big Chelsea fan, which came from my Mum, who was a mad keen supporter. We got on great as brothers, me, Lee and Gary, and any fighting and horseplay was good natured. If there was a major disagreement, the rule was you could not punch in the face. We were all mates really, though I was the boss as I was the eldest. I didn't really need to be protective of them, mind, as Lee and Gary could both look after themselves. It was just as well, as I was not the biggest, nor the most physical, of kids.

Maybe that was the reason I started going to Finchley Boxing Club at the age of 12, shortly after moving up to Ravenscroft Comprehensive School. I wanted to keep fit and learn some skills and – I'm sure – wanted to make my Dad proud. Boys do, don't they? It's the natural order of things.

My taking up the sport was certainly not at his behest. In fact, when I started, he didn't say very much. He didn't want to interfere, he would say to me later, he just wanted me to get on with things. Then one night I came home with the medical card that all amateurs must have before they are allowed to box competitively.

"Look Dad, I'm all carded up now," I said. He was stunned.

"You're actually going to do this, aren't you?" he said and I was.

From then on, once I had made my decision to box, he would become my biggest supporter and probably also my biggest critic – apart from myself. His remarks would always be constructive, though, as he knew his stuff and I would always have a great respect for his opinion.

When amateur clubs put on shows, they look to match young boxers by age, weight and experience so that there are no dangerously one-sided contests. Often they will take spare boxers, who travel for the experience, just to get a feel for the atmosphere and the occasion, but if there is an appropriate opponent, they might then get a fight. I travelled three times a 'spare' without getting a bout.

Then on the fourth occasion, on April 28th, 1995, just a few weeks short of my 13th birthday, I got a shock. It was at a working men's club in White Hart Lane, near the Tottenham Hotspur football stadium, and I thought I was just along for the ride again until I walked past a blackboard and saw my name chalked up and listed to fight. And in the first bout of the night. It was actually happening.

Perhaps the club coaches didn't want to get me nervous, perhaps they thought I would perform best if I was just thrown in at the deep end, but I didn't have any kit, no proper boxing boots, just trainers. I was given a club vest but had to borrow shorts. Dad was there – as he would be with all my fights down the years, unless there was a clash with Gary and he alternated – along with

Grandad, Lee and Gary. Uncle Dean, who was Dad's brother and would always be a big supporter of mine, was also there with his son, and my cousin, Richard.

It went pretty well, in the event, and it seemed to flash by after I had donned the headguard, which was then compulsory, and was in fact for all of my amateur career before a rule change that stopped the wearing of them. That was designed to make boxers quicker on their feet and more skilful at evading punches, rather than just standing and taking them, cushioned by the protection.

Anyway, After three fierce rounds of one and a half minutes, I had registered my first win, over a traveller who would be named on my medical card as D. Ward from a club called St Monica's, of Hoxton in East London.

Dad was as euphoric as I was and on the drive home I remember him telling me that if I got good, I could travel the world with boxing. I remember Grandad smiling and saying, recalling my Dad's amateur career: "It's starting all over again."

My next fight was in Barking, Essex against a lad called De'Ath. When we got to the venue and found out the name of my opponent, all the Finchley kids were winding me up, saying he had changed his name to Death just for me. I was worried, I have to admit, and thought I was going to take a hammering but I won well. I quickly won two more fights soon after to make it four wins from four bouts.

This boxing business was easy, wasn't it? No sweat. Just when you are even tempted to think that, though, it comes back to bite you. I would learn that, and a valuable lesson it was, in my next fight.

It was at another working men's club and next to another football ground, this time West Ham United in Green Street. It was a tough fight and I suffered my first defeat, at the hands of a lad called S. Ward from Lowestoft. Not that Grandad thought so. He never thought I lost a fight. I just got bad decisions.

More defeats followed, though. Plenty, in fact. Around my 16th birthday, I lost six out of seven bouts and it made me question whether I should go on. I didn't like getting hit and hurt at that age, of course I didn't. Who does? There was a kid at Finchley, for example, that I hated sparring with. He got me with a couple of body shots and it really hurt me.

But it wasn't really the physical pain that bothered me about boxing, or even getting knocked out, though naturally it crossed my mind. Looking back, I was a pretty game kid, after all, and gave it a good go. No, I was more worried about losing. It was the humiliation that hurt me most. I wasn't getting dropped to the canvas or stopped, and my fights were going to points decisions, but I was on the receiving end and getting punched more than I was dishing it out. I was still quite a stringy kid and wouldn't have hairs on my legs until I was 18.

Dad asked me if this was what I really wanted to do. I suppose it can't have been nice seeing your son get hit. He asked me if I wanted to take a rest for a while, which was his way of advising me to pack it in. It was my introduction to how tough boxing could be, not just in the ring. It hurt that my Dad wanted me to quit – though I knew he only wanted the best for me and for me not to get knocked about - as I was basically doing it for him. Although I would never have said that.

I reckoned that if I was going to continue, I had to get more serious and do it right. I decided I would go the best club I knew. The club where my Dad had learnt the sport properly and gone on to become a champion.

One midweek night, I packed up my kitbag without telling anyone and took the Northern Line from High Barnet down to Tottenham Court Road and changed to the Central Line for Bethnal Green. When I got out into the street, I had no idea where the Repton club was, so I asked passers-by. Eventually someone knew the way and set me out on the 10-minute walk, down the

Bethnal Green Road and turning left at Vallance Road.

After just over an hour of travelling, I got to the club, which was in the old public swimming pool and now called The Bath House, on Cheshire Street. I was a bit nervous about going in. Fortunately, I ran into someone who recognised me in Kelvin Wing, who was a club official - the junior matchmaker in fact - and had known my Dad for years. He asked me what I was doing there and I told him I wanted to join. They let me do a bit of training and gave me joining forms to take home.

I worried about going back to Finchley to tell them I was leaving, having had some good times with them. They were a good club and I had been on two amazing trips with them to Las Vegas to box against a club out there, the contests being billed as Nevada v London.

For a star-struck kid, it was great visiting the celebrated Richard Still gym in Vegas and I was awestruck seeing a young Floyd Mayweather working on the pads. Rob McCracken, who would become Carl Froch's trainer and also the Great Britain Olympic team head coach, was also there with Wayne McCulloch for a world title fight. There were lockers for various world champions. Then at one of the events one year, Evander Holyfield was ringside.

I remember the second year with less fondness, not just because I won my bout the first year and lost the next time. At the same time as we were out there, Spencer Oliver, someone I looked up to as a professional from Barnet and who would coach a bit at the Finchley gym, was fighting back home. It was against the Russian Serhiy Divakov at the Royal Albert Hall in defence of his European Super Bantamweight title and Spencer suffered a bad knockout, which required him to undergo brain surgery for a blood clot. It was a worrying time for everyone and it would end Spencer's career but thankfully he made a full recovery.

Now going back to the club after my Repton excursion,

I wanted to be straight with them and front up. I owed Finchley that. But one club official was a bit annoyed with me when I went to collect my card and I have to admit I was hurt as I rode my bike home, because I didn't want to part on bad terms. I knew I was doing the right thing, though, even at that young age.

It was going to be a long schlepp over to East London twice a week for training, sometimes even three, but I needed to find out if this was going to be the making or breaking of me. And I would not be alone for long. I was going to have support as well as company.

3

THE REPTON WAY

When you first walk into the Repton club, you can't help but be impressed by the atmosphere and the history of the place, especially when you are an impressionable teenager and steeped in boxing. In fact, many TV shows and films have used it as a location for exactly what a boxing gym should look like. The ring is at its centre and posters abound for old fight nights. A big motto hangs on the wall: NO GUTS NO GLORY. It is dusty and dirty, just how they like it. In fact, the chairman Dave Robinson once decreed that the walls should not be cleaned so as to preserve its character.

I was in awe of the place for a while. Any of the club's boxers who wins an England vest gets his framed picture on the wall and seeing all those champions, like Audley Harrison and Maurice Hope and John H. Stracey, was humbling but also inspiring. My Dad was also up there. That put an extra pressure on a young boxer but I used it to drive me on. I wanted to make sure I got up there too.

I was 16 and still very raw, a bit of a scrawny kid. I was just leaving school and glad to be. All I did, to be honest, was muck about at Ravenscroft Comp. I was only ever really interested in playing sport and I was in a mad class, where plenty bunked off regularly. I just couldn't concentrate on schoolwork, although I did all right in German funnily enough. I got a C, probably because I fancied the teacher and paid attention. Otherwise, it was mainly low grades, such as E in English and even PE. That was because I missed the practical as I was boxing in Las Vegas for Finchley.

I got into a couple of scrapes at school, one in Year 9 with a kid from the Dollis Valley estate that backed on to our school. Everyone was petrified of kids from there but I whacked one who was giving me grief and I never had any trouble after that. I never told him, never told anyone, that I was boxing at the time. There was just one other time when I hit a kid back and got caught by the headmistress. I was absolutely terrified of my Mum when I handed the letter over but she let me off on the grounds that he had hit me first.

I had been working at weekends selling fruit and veg on Barnet market and when I left, I just wanted a full-time job that would allow me time to carry on with my boxing. I managed to get a job with a cable company but it didn't last long; I thought I was going to be working in computers but as it turned out, they had me laying cables.

Then I got a job in an estate agent's in Edgware, and I remember one morning my Dad giving me a lift over in his van. Unfortunately, as we went round a corner, a tin of paint shifted and flew over me, ruining my suit. Before I could go to work, I had to go and buy a new suit in Next and Dad had to give me the money. It was probably a sign I wasn't cut out for it.

Anyway, my boxing was starting to take off, and I needed more flexible hours to give me plenty of time to train. And so I got a job working for the Post Office and had a delivery round in the West End of London, around Rathbone Place in W1. I enjoyed it. I would be up at 5 am for a 6.15 start and I loved watching London wake up. It was great as it meant I finished early and could hit the gym.

I loved Repton and was immediately proud to be a part of the club. You always felt you were part of something special when you entered the smoky gym - club officials and the trainers would still be allowed to puff on cigarettes in there at that time - and there was always a buzz. Something was always happening. There would be news, of dinners shows and upcoming fights, and when Gary started coming with me there after a few months, we would be talking excitedly all the way from the tube station wondering what we would discover that night. Lee also made a few visits but he quickly decided that boxing wasn't for him. He preferred his football.

Gary was an instant hit, even at just 12 years old, but it took a while for me to get into the Repton style. They were an elite club with so much prestige and I didn't want to let them down. I must admit I had my doubts when I lost my first fight in their famous green vest with its gold lettering, to Matthew Marsh of West Ham. Looking back it was no disgrace, though, as he went on to be an ABA champion and a British professional champion at bantamweight.

For my next fight, Kelvin Wing handed me a Repton vest that his son, also named Kelvin, had worn in winning a junior ABA title and when I won, against an S. McCoomb from Northern Ireland, I kept hold of it. It became a superstition in fact and I would wear it for every fight after that.

Over the next year, I lost only one of my next seven fights and even that was dubious, with the Dad of my opponent Ryan Barrett of the Eltham club saying he thought I had shaded it. My run even took me to the semi-finals of the Junior ABAs where I lost to Femi Fehintola of the Karmand club of Bradford.

My hero at that time as a boxer was Mike Tyson and Gary and I found out in the January of that year, 2000, that he was staying at the Grosvenor House hotel in London ahead of his fight against Julius Francis at the MEN Arena in Manchester. We were desperate for an autograph. Dad reckoned that if we went down to Park Lane early in the morning, we might just catch him coming back from a run in Hyde Park.

When we got there – me, Gary, Lee, a mate called David Beeching and Dad – we recognised a guy who was part of Tyson's entourage, a minder by the name of Steve 'Crocodile' Fitch, and he told us that we had just missed Mike. But, Crocodile added, Mike was training in a specially set up gym in the hotel and allowed a few invited guests to watch. If we came back later, we might just get lucky. So we went for some breakfast and returned at the time we were told.

As we stood there with our autograph books, Crocodile came over and picked us out and took us to the gym. He was a notorious figure, who had served time for manslaughter, but we loved him that day. As he sat us at ringside, he told us not to disturb Mike in any way during the session.

I couldn't resist it, though. When Mike came in, I took Lee's camera and asked him for a picture. He just brushed me aside, pushing me on to the chair. I was a bit taken aback but this was Mike Tyson. You didn't question him. We sat and watched but grabbed pictures of him with the flash turned off. And we got our autographs in the end.

At the time, I was just a kid who loved boxing and didn't really have an opinion on Tyson's conviction for rape. I don't think I even watched the news in those days. Clearly it was something that could not be condoned but he served his punishment, in the form of a prison sentence, and then converted to Islam so he must have felt penitent and so deserved to be able to live his life and return to boxing.

By the end of that year, 2000, I had won my first title – the National Association of Boys Clubs championships, beating Darren Lambert of Karmand at the Hilton Hotel in London. I was absolutely delighted and thought that if I had finished there I would have been happy enough. I had won a national title, which was more than I thought I would ever achieve, particularly during that spell of losing six out of seven bouts before I quit Finchley.

Gary was also making his mark and beat me to a national title in fact, earlier that year. He was silky and smooth and everyone loved to watch him. Like Dad, he was a southpaw, a boxer who favours his left hand and so leads with his right. In the first year of taking up the sport, he won England Schools title, just a month past his 13th birthday. I remember going up to the Metrodome in Barnsley on a family outing to see him win his final and felt really proud. We both felt like we were going places.

When I turned 18, I came under the tutelage of the senior head coach at Repton, Tony Burns. Tony was a wonderful character who everybody looked up to. He was such a knowledgeable figure. He would chain smoke his way through club training nights and his trademark question to everyone he met was: "Have you got any money for me?" Often he would ask complete strangers who had come in to watch. Seeing the look on their faces made everyone laugh.

On my first night at Repton, I went up to him in all innocence and asked him if he would tie my gloves up. It was a mistake and a breach of protocol. Tony just walked away. He was head coach and you didn't ask him to do such a menial task. That fell to other helpers around the place. People laughed at me and I certainly never asked again.

There was an aura about Tony and he commanded serious respect. When he talked, everyone listened. He was never really a trainer, not even a real technical coach though he had a sound technical knowledge. He never even held the pads for you to hit into, for example. But he was a guru of the sport. He planted seeds in your mind, gave you confidence. He would never praise you too highly - though later I would hear him wax lyrical about Gary - but he made you feel good about yourself.

As soon as I became a senior, Tony said that he would put me straight into the ABAs at lightweight, just for the experience. The plan was that if I came up against anyone good, he would pull me out to avoid a beating. I did a bit better than I or anyone else expected, though, and got on a roll, beating Terry Fletcher of Karmand, who was one of the favourites, in the quarter-finals.

In the semis at the Everton Leisure Centre in Liverpool, I came up against Tristan Davies of the Donnington Club in Shropshire, and it proved a really close, intense battle. In fact, it ended 17-17 on points and so it had to be decided on the complex countback system.

What happened in amateur boxing was that three of the five judges had to press their hand-held devices within one second of a clean punch landing for it to count as a point for a boxer. When it came to countback, they looked at how many times the judges had pressed their buttons in all, including outside of the one-second limit. It turned out that he edged it under that system.

It was a setback but it was my only domestic defeat of the season. In fact I only lost one other fight, that coming in a tournament in Finland after I had won my first round fight.

By now I had passed my driving test, which enabled me to take on a driving job with the Post Office. That was beneficial to my boxing, giving me more flexibility for training, and it also meant I got paid when I had an accident after going on holiday that summer following my ABA semi. In Greece with the family, I came off a motorbike and damaged my back. I could barely move for two months and was off work for almost six months in total. I still kept my email address of the time: punchingpostie@aol.com.

I had begun to feel like I was really making progress now and the England selectors had obviously taken notice of my ABA performances as I was picked for an international match against Denmark. It came too soon after the injury, though, and I was bitterly disappointed to miss out.

Fortunately, after getting back to boxing in the December of 2001, the chance came again soon after when I was picked for a tournament in Hungary to fight at the 63.5 Kilograms weight, having filled out since reaching the ABA semis at 60Kgs.

I was delighted and began dreaming of wearing that England vest, like my Dad had. The team flew to Budapest, then had to take a two-hour coach trip to the venue, at Debrecen. I could see immediately this was serious stuff, with so many talented boxers there. I was a bit overwhelmed at first, just a kid making his international debut. The Russians in particular seemed an intimidating bunch.

At the start of each day of the tournament, like all of the tournaments I would go on to with England in fact, there would be a team meeting and a ceremonial presentation of a new vest for each round you made it through. Your team-mates would applaud and I remember bursting with pride.

In football, it's a cap. In boxing it's a prized vest. Now I would be joining my Dad, and Audley and Co, on the walls at Repton. Even if I lost, I had my England vest.

But I didn't lose. In fact, I began to put a great run together. I won my international debut fight against local favourite Jozsef Gerebecz by 15-9 and rang Dad that night to tell him, feeling so proud. In turn, he said he was proud of me. It felt good to hear how happy he was for me.

I was now in the semi-finals and there I beat a Slovakian, Andrej Sarkozy, this time getting the benefit of the countback rule after the judges' scores had come in at 19-19. I had exceeded my own expectations and had a silver medal at least. I thought that would probably be what I would end up with as my opponent was Yuri Ramanau of Belarus, who was six years older than me and had 25 international bouts. As a pro, he would go on to beat good English fighters in Bobby Vanzie, who became British and Commonwealth lightweight champion, and Steve Murray.

My performance was pure gold, though, as I beat him well on points, by 21 to 13. I jumped for joy at the verdict. I thought I had won it but until you get the announcement, you are always nervous. I couldn't wait to ring home. My conversation with Dad after the first round, filled with understated pride, now turned into a loud, thrilled exchange.

After making the call, I hit the town with my team-mates and took advantage of lager being the equivalent of around 60 pence for a large Stein. There was just one snag. The next morning we had an early coach the next morning to get back to Budapest airport and I was out for the count when it came time to leave. The team manager Paul King banged on my door and woke me up. He was good about it, though, making me a black coffee and saying I had deserved my celebration.

When we got back to Stansted, I was taken aback by my welcoming committee. There was every possible Barker in the arrivals hall, including uncles and cousins, as well as plenty of my mates. They had even laid on a limousine to take me home to Barnet. I couldn't stomach the Champagne on offer, though, after my excess of the previous night.

The win gave me confidence as a boxer and probably as a person too. I met my partner Gemma around that time, in a night-club in Enfield, and there was an instant attraction. She was with a group of mates, and so was I. You know the scene. A few days later I asked a mate to get her number for me from one of her mates that he knew and rang her to ask her out.

She was studying graphic design at a college in St Albans at the time and the rest would become history... a history that would involve our having two kids together, Scarlett Rose and Charlie. She's had to show some stickability over the years being with a boxer and seeing him at his very worse, banged up physically and emotionally. It must also have something to do with the deep love between us.

It was on the back of the Hungary tournament that I was picked for England for the Commonwealth Games in Manchester in 2002. It was a bit of a surprise to the boxing community, I think, as Lenny Daws was the ABA champion and he was older and more experienced than me.

But Tony Burns had been advancing my cause and the selectors took notice of him. He had earned that respect from the sport's authorities. He was quite simply the best judge of a boxer in the country for years and years and the best at producing champions. In fact, many people at the time considered him the Sir Alex Ferguson of amateur boxing.

I didn't know Lenny at all then but word got back to me that he was not happy. I don't suppose I would have been in his situation, either. Later, we would become friends. At that time, I just couldn't let any controversy over my selection affect me. I had a major tournament to prepare for and I was determined to take my chance.

4

GOING FOR GOLD

It was the day before the Commonwealth Games of 2002 began in Manchester and the England boxing team was gathered in the games village at Manchester University after training. It was press day and all the media were there - television, radio and all the papers.

One by one, the boxers were interviewed. All except me. I got angrier and angrier the longer I sat there on my own and they ignored me. Clearly nobody expected anything from me and probably thought I was a bit of an anonymous no-hoper. "Bloody hell," I thought. "I'm going to show you lot."

I had been very nervous ahead of the Games and there had been that bit of controversy within the sport about my selection, so I was in a feisty mood anyway. It didn't help watching everyone such as the weightlifters eat what they wanted at the 24-hour restaurant in the village while I was minding my diet to stay within the 63.5 Kgs limit, which equated to light welterweight.

Now, with my snubbing by the media, it felt like every bit of outside pressure was taken away from me. There was just the pressure that I would always put on myself. I could really go about it now. I settled down, feeling comfortable that I had other Repton boxers around me. My room-mate was welterweight Danny Happe, probably my best mate at the club at that time, and another welterweight, Tony Cesay, was representing Sierra Leone, the country of his parents' birth.

I certainly felt well prepared, along with the rest of the England team. We had all got to know each other first on a bonding trip to Austria, staying in log cabins out in the sticks. It was a mixture of perspiration and inspiration, along with some good laughs.

The perspiration came from some tough physical work – though nowhere near the three intense training camps we would have leading up to the Games at Peterlee in County Durham, Crystal Palace and Manchester. The inspiration came in a brilliant video they showed us of English athletes winning medals at previous Games, to a soundtrack of U2's It's A Beautiful Day. It was very emotional and I really wanted some of it for myself.

The laughs came first in a canoe slalom we were all asked to take part in. I was put in a boat - is that the right word? – with Darran Langley, a light-flyweight who had beaten me when I was a kid at Finchley. Maybe we didn't have enough weight in the canoe, what with him being so small, but we went off course and ended up a mile down stream until we managed to get out. It was a long walk back.

Another night, we watched the film The Blair Witch Project in the community room at the complex. We were in log cabins in the middle of nowhere, remember. We were all pretty tense and intent on the screen and didn't notice Danny Happe creep into the room. He was wearing a black motorcycle helmet and went over to Matthew Marsh, tapping him on the shoulder. Matthew turned round and nearly jumped out of his skin. It was a good job Danny was wearing the helmet otherwise he might have got chinned.

My first fight at the Wythenshawe Forum, where the preliminary fights for the Games were held, turned out to be my toughest, against Paul McCloskey of Northern Ireland, who would go on to be British and European champion at the weight. It was a close contest for a long time but I pulled away, landing well with my jab, to prevail on points by 20-15. Then came a stoppage against Roy Sheldon of Jamaica on the 'outclassed' rule - which applies when one of the fighters is being beaten too easily and is to spare him punishment – to put me in the quarter final.

I was nervous before that, knowing that a win would put me in the semis and guarantee me a medal - and also because my Ghanaian opponent, Lartei Lartey, had knocked out his opponent in reaching the last eight. In the end, though, it was a comfortable enough 24-8 win.

I was absolutely delighted, and even more so when I got some news on my way to the weigh-in ahead of my semi-final, against Davidson Emenogu of Nigeria. "He's pulled out," an official told me and I soon found out that the guy had broken his foot playing football in a kick-about in the Games village.

Now I was in the final, guaranteed a silver. I had some sympathy for the Nigerian bloke but playing football was a bit daft so close to such a big fight. I liked my football and as well as supporting Chelsea, I played a bit for East Barnet Old Grammarians – the EBOGS – as a midfield player mainly who liked to score the odd goal. I would not have dared in the run-up to this, though. Still, I was happy to take all the luck going.

Finals day was in the huge MEN Arena, which meant I got to fight in the same venue as Mike Tyson when he beat Julius Francis. My final was to be against a Ugandan, Mohammed Kayongo, who was captain of their entire team and had carried the country's flag in the opening ceremony. Tony Burns took the chance to have a word with me beforehand.

"I've just had Harry Lawson on the phone," he said, referring to an old Repton boxer.

"Yeah?" I said.

"He made it to a Commonwealth Games final once," said Tony. "He lost. He's told me to make sure to tell you that it still winds him up that he never won the gold."

That was Tony. He planted seeds. Made you think. It was great motivation as he knew that more than getting hurt or any other consideration, what I hated most was losing and the fear of it always spurred me on.

It was a tough contest and although I got the upper hand early on and led by six points, Kayongo came back with a couple of right hands in the second round that caught me. In the end, even though I knew I had not boxed as well as I could, I came through by 18 points to 14.

I remember sinking to my knees when it was announced and then seeing my Mum in the audience crying. The whole family was there – Dad, Grandad, Lee, Gary and little Daisy, as well as Uncle Dean of course - but it was Mum I picked out. It was the first time she had been to see me fight as she hated the idea of seeing me and Gary get hit. We had been to New York earlier in the year with Repton for a tournament - it was not long after 9/11 and visiting Ground Zero was a humbling experience with the city still raw – and although Mum came on the trip, she did not come to see me and Gary fight.

It took a lot for her to be there then, and I felt so proud. In fact, it suddenly came home to me just how big a reason making my family proud played in my boxing.

Standing on the podium with the gold medal around my neck was a wonderful moment that I knew I would treasure for ever and I fought back the tears. I was the first Englishman to win gold at the boxing tournament. We had four other finalists but only one other gold medallist, in David Dolan at super heavyweight, with Darran Langley, Paul Smith and Steven Birch taking silver.

I also found out that Tony Burns had vowed to other people at Repton that he would give up smoking if I won the gold. He was as good as his word and never smoked again.

Now the TV, radio and press all wanted to know plenty about me, which put a wry smile on my face, and now I could bask in the glory of gold. I got whisked off to the BBC studios to be interviewed by Sue Barker. I would get better as an interviewee down the years but I was tongue-tied in those days and it was a bit embarrassing. I was still a bit of a gawky 20-year-old, 5ft 11in tall now, and not that confident. In fact, I was a bit in awe of one of the great figures in British broadcasting, having always watched her on *A Question of Sport*. It is ironic that later in my career I would be on the show myself as a guest.

Now I could give that 24-hour canteen a caning and I ate very well, loving watching all the great athletes come and go around the place, like Jonathan Edwards, Kelly Holmes, Paula Radcliffe and local favourite Darren Campbell. There was also a long walkway from the security gate to the village itself and they put plaques down for all the medallists. It was a real thrill seeing 'Gold: Darren Barker. Boxing. 63.5Kg.'

The whole experience made me determined to go further and try for the Athens Olympic Games of 2004. I had ideas of turning professional in the future, and had been introduced by Tony Burns to a trainer he trusted by the name of Tony Sims, should I ever want to make the step; what is called in boxing 'turning over'. He seemed like a genuine guy and we hit it off straight away. I even went to the gym he rented at Woodford Rugby Club in Essex to spar a few times, along with Gary, who was developing well alongside me.

For now, with my style still geared towards scoring points rather than hurting opponents as in the pros, and with my body still developing, I wanted to see how far I could go as an amateur. And I was doing pretty well financially, thanks to lottery money, by being a part of the England set-up. The previous September, in fact, I had received a letter from the ABA saying that I was now being included on their World Class programme and would be funded by Sport England. That had given me quite a boost.

I actually had no need to work now as I was getting £1,281 a month clear. I will always remember the figure. Before the Commonwealth Games, we were all on £750 a month. On the back of the gold, my money had gone up by more than £500. David Haye, who would go on to be World Heavyweight Champion, also joined the team at that time and he was on more than any of us. I suppose his food bills were higher.

Pre-Athens, the governing bodies changed the weights and I moved up from light-welterweight to welter, where the limit was 69Kgs, increased from 67Kgs. It suited me down to the ground and I was picked for the World Championships in Bangkok in 2003. That was another great experience for a young kid, not least being in a bar and seeing an elephant being led past the open window. And being billeted next to a running track where there were so many people jogging that you couldn't see the track.

I started badly, being decked early on in my first fight against the Japanese Koji Sato. I switched off as I was coasting and got caught and punished for it. I was fine, though, and after taking the count of eight, I went on to win by 31 points to 22 after the four two-minute rounds. After that came a win over a South African, Kwanene Zulu, the ref stopping it in the second when I was well on top.

Now I was in the last eight, just one win away from a medal, but I was up against a real pedigree fighter in the American Andre Berto, who would go on to be a highly impressive world champion at the weight as a professional.

I boxed really well, giving one of the best performances of my amateur career, and was seven points up going into the last round. I did well then, I thought, to keep at bay the inevitable rally he put together in the last round and waited for the referee to raise my arm when it was time for the verdict.

I could not believe it then when the judges announced that I had lost 24-22. Berto may well have won the last round but never in a million years by nine points. I was devastated and disgusted. You know as a boxer when you have won or lost and I knew I had won. Just that win would have guaranteed me at least a bronze medal. In the World Championships. Imagine – a world bronze.

To show the standard of competition, by the way, the middleweight division was won by Gennady Golovkin of Kazakhstan who would go on to become the most feared boxer in the professional middleweight division, taking over from the legendary Sergio Martinez, who would play a big part in my career. On the way in that tournament, Golovkin would beat the Romanian Lucian Bute, who would become a professional world champion himself at super middleweight and have such a battle with Carl Froch.

The defeat took the wind out of my sails as an amateur and to be honest, I lost a bit of stomach for the sport. I was competing and still wanting to make my family proud but just didn't have the same motivation. I reckoned I had already achieved a lot. I was getting older and settling into my relationship with Gemma and enjoying playing football for EBOGS, even though I was a rubbish penalty taker and couldn't score one to save my life, shown when we once lost a cup final.

I was also getting too big for the 69Kgs division but was too small really for the next weight up in the new divisions, 75Kgs, which was middleweight. But that was the weight I was allocated to try and qualify for the Olympics.

I was sent to the European Championships in Croatia in February 2004 and beat an Italian, Andrea Di Luisa, by 32 points to 20, in the first round. Now I had just two more wins to record to reach the semi-finals and guarantee a place in the British team for Athens. The problem was, the other guys were bigger than me. For the only time in my career, I was not having trouble making the weight.

In the last 16, I came up against Ireland's Andy Lee, who would go on to be a world middleweight champion himself. I was always forcing the fight after falling a few points behind early on and Andy was a good counter-puncher. In the end, he won 18-8 and would go on to win a highly commendable bronze medal.

It meant I had to try again at one of the other Olympic qualifying tournaments that Spring and I was sent to Gothenburg, Sweden in the April. My first fight, though, proved to be my last as an amateur. It was a bad draw, against the highly rated Hungarian Karoly Balzsay, and I was stopped on the outclassed rule in the third round. It was the only time in my amateur career that it happened to me. At least I managed to stay on my feet. Balzsay would go on to reach the last 16 in Athens and then turn pro and become WBA Super Middleweight Champion.

I can remember crying afterwards in the dressing room. I knew my Olympic dreams were over and to be honest, I knew then my amateur career was over. I was 22 years old and couldn't face going through all this again only to have my hopes dashed after four more years of struggle, hoping I might qualify for the next Games in Beijing. In the end, nobody was selected for Athens to represent Great Britain at middleweight and in fact just one boxer was selected at any weight – Amir Khan.

I hoped that Beijing would be Gary's time. As my amateur career was ending, his was really going up a level and I was delighted for him. The previous July, he had gone to Louisiana in the United States to represent Great Britain at the Junior Olympic Games – with Grandad Rodney and cousin Richard as company – and only gone and come back with a gold medal, beating the Puerto Rican Luis Orlando Del Valle in the 54Kgs final. Del Valle later became an American citizen and became their number one ranked amateur before having a good professional career.

What also showed Gary's quality was that in the same tournament, Amir Khan also won gold by outclassing the American Victor Ortiz, who would go on to be a world champion at welterweight as a professional at welterweight.

The best part of Gary's amateur career still lay ahead of him but mine had come and gone and I came to terms with that as I watched Amir Khan win a silver medal at lightweight in Athens. I was delighted for him but had mixed emotions. I was sad that it was over but relieved at the same time. I was done.

My domestic record showed only 13 defeats from 68 fights and there were many more international fights that took my number of bouts to over a century. It had been a good career and I had enjoyed myself, getting to travel to some amazing places wearing an England vest.

It was just a shame I didn't get that world bronze but I knew the time was right to move on. But what to do now? I could work for my Dad in his painting and decorating business. Or I could take up Tony Sims's offer to turn pro with him and see if I was any good. In the event, I would end up doing both…

5

TONY – 1

Tony Sims was born in Bethnal Green in 1961 and grew up in a block of flats opposite the Repton Boxing Club. Now the area is almost, if not quite, gentrified as moneyed London spreads its wings. Then it was among the toughest of neighbourhoods, breeding the toughest of people. Including the Kray twins.

Tony's Dad took him to Repton when he was 11 and after that came a spell at the St George's club in Stepney. When he left school, he got a job as an apprentice mechanic at Vauxhall Bridge and so fought for the local Fitzroy Lodge club. Boxing helped him, he says, through the difficult teenage years. He had around 60 fights and represented London.

A mate's Dad got Tony a job at Billingsgate fish market as a scale boy, weighing up prawns and shrimps, starting at 4am. After a year, at the age of 18, he got his licence as a fish porter. There was good money in it but the work was physically demanding.

Tony boxed till he was 22 and wanted to be a pro, sparring at light middleweight with big faces of the 80s, Terry Marsh and Nigel Benn, but drifted away from the sport for a while until he began to help out at the gym of a friend, Peter DeFreitas, who was Benn's manager. Tony acquired a trainer's licence of his own and DeFreitas gave him a couple of fighters he had on his books to work with.

Tony rented some space at Wanstead Rugby Club in Essex to set up a gym and made his first signing from the amateur ranks, a lad called Steve Smith, who would soon change his name.

"He saw a medium," says Tony. "She told him he was a gladiator in a

former life. So he changed his name to Steve Spartacus. He had blond hair and blue eyes and used to wear these cheap Roman togas in the ring. He won 16 fights in a row and became English champion then got beat for the British. He became my friend and had a decent career before retiring."

That was the pleasure for Sims - finding amateurs and polishing them into good pros - but the money was not yet coming in. That was coming from the pub he ran in Buckhurst Hill, The T Bar and the small boxing shows he promoted at the Prince Regent Hotel in Chigwell.

He kept his eye on the Repton conveyor belt, had a good relationship with the head coach there, Tony Burns and his son, Tony Burns junior, with whom he also ran a removals business. He was the man on the spot to whom Darren Barker turned when the time came to become professional.

What neither Tony nor Darren knew at that time, was that he would come to be more than a boxing trainer for Darren. Because, through a personal tragedy of his own that he would later reveal, he would be able to relate to him on a human level too. It would become a relationship that was meant to be, as Tony would discover…

"I was always really interested in Darren and went up to see him win the Commonwealth Games gold medal. He would then come to my gym a couple of times a week to train and we got him sparring with pros. He was not the fittest at that time. Being a pro is a different thing altogether.

When he knew he had done everything he could in the amateurs and was ready to turn over, I was ready to offer him a deal. There was no signing-on money but we got him a sponsored Mini, me and Tony Burns junior, and he signed with me and the promoter I worked with, Mick Hennessey. Mick really liked Darren as well and he had a deal early on at the BBC, before he went on to work with Sky then ITV. It was a great signing and a great deal all round.

We had to work hard early on to change his style from amateur to pro. It is a different sport. One is about just scoring points and getting away. You can get 10 points up by landing some punches then not let the other bloke anywhere near you.

In the pros, the rewards are bigger for trying to hurt people and knock them down. You're trying to win rounds 10-9, or 10-8 with a knockdown. You need power, speed and stamina. If you're going to be a champion, you've got to prepare for 12 three-minute rounds, not four at two minutes, or three of three minutes these days.

Mick had some misgivings early on about Darren's amateur style. Most amateurs don't have great head movement as they don't need to learn it because they wear headguards and are a bit too upright. Some even pull their head back.

But then I took Mick with me to watch Darren spar with Gilbert Eastman, who was then the Southern Area champion, and Darren absolutely boxed his head off. I remember Mick saying: "You're right. He could be a good fighter." He was a light middleweight then. Couldn't make the weight at welter but was too small for middle.

Gary used to come to the gym with Darren too and Darren won't mind me saying it but Gary was different class. Brilliant. I've had some fighters through my doors down the years but that kid was the most naturally gifted kid that ever walked in. When you saw him, it was like a dream. He could change his style easily from amateur to professional.

I'll give you an example. I used to take Gary out sparring to other gyms with his brother and I remember a good friend and fellow trainer Rob McCracken ringing me up asking for someone to come and work his fighter Lee Meager.

Lee was British lightweight champion at the time. Gary was 18 and had just won the Commonwealth juniors. He wasn't even in training really but I just said: "Gaz, go for the experience. See how many rounds you can do." He agreed, was also up for something like that.

This is how natural a boxer he was… He did eight rounds with him. He sparred beautifully and showed so much skill against a good champion. Rob said to me that he was the best kid he had ever seen and he has seen some, in his role as a pro trainer for Carl Froch, and with the London 2012 Olympic team. When I look back, I thought that if he was doing that at 18, what's he going to do in the Oympics or when he turns pro?

I am convinced he would have gone to the Beijing Olympics in 2008 and if and when he had gone pro, he would have been a world champion. Without a doubt.

It wasn't difficult for Darren knowing all that, though. They are not the sort of family that has rivalries. That's the lovely thing about the Barker family. They support each other. All I ever saw was encouragement, one for the other.

Don't get me wrong. Darren was class, too. I made other signings but he was my best. It was just that he would have to work at it. It was always work, work, work with him.

I didn't see it early on until it all happened, and I really got to know Darren, and we talked about the things that had happened in my life, but he walked that fine line where he was prone to depressions. It's like a lot of talented sports people isn't it?

Early on, while I knew he was good and that I could make him better, I didn't know just what a real talent he was. One of the problems with Darren would always be as well that he didn't know just what a talent he was. I did know I was lucky to be working with that talent as he started to emerge as a really good pro. ”

6

GOING PRO

People see professional boxers on TV and think they are making fortunes. It's just not true unless and until you get the big fights, the world title fights, and even then I think people might be surprised at what a challenger might get, certainly at some of the smaller weights where the public and TV interest is not so high. In fact, when you add up the hours some boxers rack up in training and then match it to what they get on the night, especially when they are starting out, it probably adds up to less than the minimum wage.

The carrot, though, is always that world championship. That fight for a title, or the defence of a title, that can set you up for life. There is also the lure of the bright lights, the chance for a bit of fame and glory. Add into the mix the addictive way the sport can get under your fingernails and the decision to turn pro for me became a simple one. What else did I know, anyway? It seemed the logical next step.

I have always been lucky with the people who advised me on my boxing. First there was my Dad, who always gave me such sound advice both from a technical viewpoint and as a mentor, then came Tony Burns, head coach at Repton.

For this next phase of my career, Tony Sims was just the right man. He liked my ability and reckoned he could turn me into a pro. I hit it off with him straight away. He was honest and spoke my language. He was also building a decent stable, with Steve

Spartacus, Butch Lesley and Andrew Lowe at light heavyweight, Daniel Cadman at super middleweight and Dave Stewart at lightweight.

Dad had some reservations about me turning pro, probably the natural paternal ones about simply wanting the best for his son. We were concerned about the stories you hear about the fight game being corrupt and he was worried about me getting ripped off. I was willing to take my chances, though. I was grateful to Dad for the opportunity to work as a painter and decorator with him but it was just to keep me ticking over and I didn't want to do it for the rest of my life.

Not that I could give up some casual work with him just yet. My money from Sport England on quitting as an amateur naturally dried up immediately and there was no big signing-on fee. I wasn't Amir Khan, after all, fresh from showing himself so marketable in Athens. I was grateful, though, for a sponsored Mini and a small monthly wage from a sponsor Tony had, the John Knight Construction Company, that covered my expenses travelling from Barnet to Tony's gym at the Wanstead rugby club near Epping Forest every weekday.

I think Dad was reassured when he met Tony Sims. Tony introduced me to Mick Hennessy, who was promoting his boxers along with some others that included an up-and-coming super middleweight called Carl Froch, who had just won the Commonwealth professional title. Tony and Mick both told us the good and the bad about the professional sport and its people, so we were forewarned and forearmed. It didn't put me off and I made my own decision. I was ready for it all, including the business side.

Tony set about fine-tuning my style, which I heard a few doubters in the amateur sport were saying would not transfer well. I had always boxed off the back foot, my aim being to work off the jab, land clean, if not necessarily forceful, punches and score points for the judges. Now he wanted me to be more on the front foot, stamping my authority on my opponent in the first round, making sure I got my front foot round the outside of a rival's to make it easier to get in a powerful right-hander.

Tony was right. I was discovering it was a different sport. I guess I was a bit like a semi-professional non-League footballer who may have won trophies but was now going up into the League to be a full-timer. Even if I was still on non-League money.

In fact, I spent the first six months after turning pro – early in the spring of 2004 - in the gym being schooled until my first fight in the early autumn. The wait for my debut was mainly because several potential opponents fell by the wayside. But it was not time wasted and a grounding I look back on with both fondness and gratitude.

I loved the camaraderie of the gym, even if it doing this on a daily basis took some getting used to. This was my job now. That began to hit home with me. And it was lovely having Gary accompanying me regularly and training and sparring alongside me. Naturally he impressed everyone. These days, he was boxing in my lucky Repton vest that I had handed down to him. I looked forward to the day, after he had won his Olympic gold medal, when he was my professional stablemate.

The delay in finding an opponent also meant I was hungry for action when Howard Clarke finally took up the gauntlet. He would be facing a boxer now with the professional name of 'Dazzling' Darren Barker. It was a natural nickname that came from days as a 12-year-old kid in the back garden when the World Wrestling Federation was becoming big and we all fancied ourselves as superstars as we grappled amongst ourselves. We all had to have nicknames and my schoolmate Stephen Patten gave me 'Dazzling', which stuck.

The bout, on Friday 24th September, took place the day after Howard's 37th birthday and while he may have been past his best, he was still a class act. He had, after all, fought the American-

Mexican Fernando Vargas for the IBF World Light Middleweight title at the spiritual home of the sport in Madison Square Garden, New York, five years earlier.

I was buzzing for it. It was a big night at the Ice Arena in Nottingham, Carl Froch's home town, where he was king of the hill and top of the bill, and live on a BBC channel, though the punters and television hardly got value for money as Carl would retain his Commonwealth Super Middleweight title and win the vacant British title by knocking out Derby's Damon Hague in the first round. I was also live on TV, even if down the undercard, as I had a bit of a name after having won the Commonwealth gold medal.

I had been a bit taken aback in the run-up to the fight when Tony told me that it was going to be six three-minute rounds, having been used to four two-minute rounds in the amateurs. I was expecting four by three minutes. I was nervous about whether I might last the distance but Tony told me that I was fit enough – and I felt it too. A sign of my fitness, in fact, was that I didn't even count down the rounds and I now look back and wonder what I was worried about, even if I did feel a bit tired for the last couple of minutes.

In the event, I dominated all six rounds and won comfortably, getting a unanimous decision from the three judges. I was careful to follow what Tony had instructed me to do and get on the front foot then let the shots go. I was delighted. I had won a fight as a professional. With each milestone, I was achieving more than I had ever believed possible.

The menfolk in the family all made the trip up, along with a big posse of mates, as they would always do as my career unfolded. I also earned money for the first time – £4,000. Six months work for four grand. What was that about the minimum wage? It didn't matter to me a lot at the time. I was off and running, a fully fledged pro now.

Tony wanted to keep me as active as possible and within six weeks I was back in the ring again, against the Welshman David White. I was excited to be on home territory, at Wembley Conference Centre, and around 100 of my growing support in Barnet made the short trip to see me fight at light middleweight. I weighed 156 pounds, still a lad filling out and finding his proper weight and four pounds under what I would settle at as a middleweight.

I was bottom of the bill, which would be topped by Junior Witter, who would win the European Super Lightweight title that night. There was a group of us from Tony's gym, with Steve Spartacus and Daniel Cadman also having outings. It was another BBC fight night, among the last pro boxing events they covered.

This time it was supposed to be four rounds but I still had nerves, this time due to a burden of expectation I was starting to shoulder. I expected a lot of myself and I didn't want to let down all my family and friends and what was a home venue. I needn't have worried too much. It went only two rounds before the stoppage that would have David deciding it would be his last fight.

I stayed in training, was always in training at that time in fact, though it would take another four months for me to get back into the ring, mainly because opponents kept pulling out through injury. The Barker family still had plenty of boxing to occupy them, though. And to cheer and celebrate.

Accompanied by my Grandad Rodney and cousin Richard, Gary travelled out to Australia, to Bendigo in Victoria, north of Melbourne, for the Junior Commonwealth Games. Fighting at 60Kgs, Gary breezed through his bouts, beating David McComb of Northern Ireland, then David Appleby of Scotland in the final, to win gold for England.

He was in good company. James DeGale, who would go on to win gold at the Beijing Olympics and fight as a pro for the IBF World Super Middleweight title, also won gold at 75Kgs, while Repton team-mate Ryan Pickard won at 69Kgs. Ryan would always remain amateur and became the club's captain and a great mate to Gary and me.

Home came the hero and we had a fantastic family Christmas. Both Gary and I felt our boxing careers were really on a roll.

The first few months of the new year of 2005 were a bit frustrating as I waited for my next fight. Mick Hennessy had lost his BBC deal and it would be another few months before he did a new one with Sky. So Tony got me on a bill at Hackney Empire in East London, which was an interesting venue. It was the first time it had been used for boxing.

Even on the day before my scheduled March date, another opponent withdrew. Champing at the bit - and needing to earn some money – I was grateful that Leigh Wicks agreed to stand in at the last minute, having got a call while out shopping with his family in his native Brighton. Leigh is one of those journeymen without whom boxing would not survive. He was nearly 40 at the time and his experience and ringcraft would be a good test as I looked to build my record.

To be honest, I was too young and strong for him and he just wasn't at my fitness level in a fight that would force him into the decision that it was time to call it a day. It was stopped in the fourth of the six two-minute rounds, to the appreciation of another good crowd of supporters who had followed me over to the East End. I was now at three fights, three wins.

I would stretch that to seven unbeaten fights by the end of what would be a busy year, during which I even fought twice in a week at one point.

Just two weeks later came my first foreign opposition in the shape of Andrei Sherel of Belarus at Brentwood Leisure Centre, my fourth different venue in four fights. This bill was organised by Tony himself, with my need to keep fighting and Mick Hennessy still not doing shows unless they were going to be televised.

It turned out to be my third stoppage of an opponent in a row, this time in the third round. It was all going smoothly. Except that my next fight three months later would see me encounter the first of the injuries that I would seem to be prone to.

It was another Carl Froch bill in Nottingham – with Mick now having his Sky deal – on which he would beat Matthew Barney and so successfully defend his British and Commonwealth Super Middleweight titles, against Ernie Smith of Stourport, another of those honest journeymen who would accept fights at short notice and who would end up fighting 161 times in his career. His fight against me was his 100th as a professional, for which he received an award from the British Boxing Board of Control that night.

Ernie, in fact, would fight every few weeks as a trial horse for up-and-comers, and a couple of months earlier had been matched against a young Sheffield boxer by the name of Kell Brook. Kell, who would go on to be a world champion, at welterweight, had prevailed on points after six rounds and I did the same. The problem was, though, that in throwing a left hand, I damaged some ligaments. Ernie had a head of iron. After that, I could barely use it again and desperately tried to score with just my right hand. It was agony any time I threw my left out.

I would be shocked, incidentally, to learn of the suicide of Ernie just under five years later at the age of just 31, not long after he had been turned down for a renewal of his licence following an MRI scan and losing 55 fights in a row. His twin brother Billy, who apparently never really recovered from his brother's death, also took his own life a few years after that. It was all really sad.

Despite my sore left hand, I took another fight just a week later that summer, against Sheffield's Dean Walker at the Prince Regent Hotel in Chigwell, Essex and won again on points, but at a cost. I was still in pain and four fights in four months were also taking a toll on me mentally. I needed a break and Tony agreed.

It took me to Ibiza with a mate, Ben 'Boff' Levy, just for a few days but it didn't end well. After a couple of good days and nights in San Antonio, we went for a quiet couple of drinks at a bar but somehow got caught up in a drinking game with some group and slept through the alarm for our flight the next morning. Renting the room for one more day and buying another flight home cost me plenty of my hard-earned money.

It was December before I had another payday, with the arm now feeling better. It was on another Carl Froch bill in Nottingham, Carl beating Ruben Groenewald of South Africa to retain his Commonwealth title. I was up against Brighton's John Paul Temple and came through with a stoppage in the final – sixth – round to end the year on a high.

It had been a lively first full year as a professional, a really good learning experience and I was earning decent if not spectacular money, getting a flat sum per fight of around £4,000 to £5,000 depending on the size of the promotion, then a percentage of the tickets that I managed to sell, my brother Lee taking charge of that. The money would all go through Tony, who would then deduct his cut and pass the balance on to me.

I would always replay the fights in my mind afterwards and would struggle to sleep, lying awake in my bed at Nan and Grandad's. The next day after a fight, I would be shattered but in a satisfied kind of way. In fact, it was a good year personally as Gemma and I built our relationship further and a satisfying year again professionally for me and for Gary, whose amateur career just kept getting better and better.

For that year, he won the junior ABA title in convincing style, beating Carl Howes of Stevenage in the final, to emulate Dad and confirm himself as one of the rising stars of the British scene. We were all delighted for him and it meant another Christmas dinner where we could savour our progress. None of us could know that it would be the last Christmas we would all be together.

7

END OF THE INNOCENCE

I have always loved York Hall in Bethnal Green. It is a proper cockpit of a boxing venue with an upstairs gallery looking down on the ring and the place really rocks with fans who know the sport. Downstairs there is a noisy bar and seating that feels as if it comes right up to the ropes, giving it an intimate, almost claustrophobic feel.

I had experienced the unique atmosphere of one of the great British venues as an amateur with Repton, with it being our local hall, and now I was to get plenty of experience of it as a pro. In fact, I would fight there four times in just six months as I built my record and began to get noticed, with Mick Hennessy's TV deal, now with Sky, bringing me to a wider audience.

The East End fans particularly seem to like a Friday night tear-up, getting dressed up for the boxing before going on for a proper night out, and my first outing of 2006, against Richard Mazurek from Leamington Spa, was a good example as we got an appreciative reception for providing eight rounds of entertainment.

It was the first time I had fought that many rounds and I was again concerned about my stamina but I came through on a unanimous decision in good style in the end, despite him being an awkward opponent. It turned out it was Richard's 29th birthday that night but I was in no mood to give out presents.

It was probably after my next fight, just four weeks later, that people in the sport began to look at me with new eyes, accepting that I was successfully making the transition from amateur to professional and was a proper prospect. Having been a light middleweight, my next fight, against the Frenchman Louis Mimoune, was made at middleweight, which Tony always thought would be where I would settle. It is a classic division, 160lbs – 11 stones 6 lbs – a weight which has been set in stone since 1884.

By now I was moving up the undercard and was second only to Carl Froch, who successfully defended his Commonwealth title by stopping Dale Westerman of Australia.

The experienced Mimoune, who had just turned 31, came to England with a decent pedigree but I was quickly into my stride and he never really had a chance. With 10 seconds left of the second round, the referee stepped in to stop him taking further punishment and I was a winner again.

Three months later, I recorded my first knockout, seeing off Danny Thornton from Yorkshire in another middleweight fight, in the sixth round, on a bill which would see Lenny Daws and Lee Meager win vacant British titles. It was a satisfying night, taking me into double figures for consecutive wins, but perhaps it made me a bit complacent for my next fight in the July on a Wednesday night Sky bill, one that would almost stop me in my tracks. It certainly taught me plenty of professional lessons – the hard way.

It was against Conroy McIntosh of Wolverhampton and I was expected to win comfortably given that he had lost his previous nine fights. But things would not go to plan, with the evening getting off to a bad start. I was told that I was going to be third fight on but due to somebody being late, I was asked to go on first and I was cold going into the ring, having had to put the gloves on quickly.

McIntosh was such a big lump, a beast of a bloke, and hard to handle. Come the second round, I got caught with an absolute kisser and got decked. What I would call proper decked. It was as clean a hit as you could imagine, a right hand coming from low down and catching me flush on the chin. Suddenly I didn't know where I was.

I staggered to my feet, though, still hurting from the shot, but ridiculously I got caught again almost straight away and was knocked over once more. I had to dig deep just to get to my feet but I managed it and was proud of the way I did. Later I heard that Gary had left when he saw me getting battered but returned when he heard the cheers for me getting up the second time.

Though it did not feel like it immediately after the fight when I was embarrassed – and certainly not at the time when I was just trying to survive – the experience would stand me in good stead for the rest of my career. And one fight in particular that everyone would come to remember me for.

Gradually I got myself together and made it to the end of the round. Tony was quickly in my ear and after a drenching with water, I returned to my senses. Now focused, I went back out there and let my boxing take over. I won the next round and the next after that. Gradually I got myself on top.

By the seventh of the scheduled eight rounds, I was even enjoying myself. I had shown I could recover and then dominate a fight. As I wore McIntosh down, the referee stepped in to stop the contest. My enjoyment seemed to be mirrored by Sky, with the production people telling me it had gone down well with the viewing public. That was encouraging, but I didn't want too many more nights like that.

After that, it was a step up in class and venue in the September, to Alexandra Palace and my first title fight as a professional, for the vacant Southern Area Middleweight title, against Hussain Osman. He was a real tough cookie, who was born in Syria but based in Paddington. It was on the same bill as Junior Witter fighting for the vacant WBC Light Welterweight title, which he would claim by outpointing DeMarcus Corley of the United States.

I was excited beforehand with so many of my supporters

making the trip of just a few miles across North London and because it was a title I really wanted to win due to an experience I had had as a teenager. When I was just 14, I went to watch my fellow Barnet boxer Spencer Oliver win the Southern Area title, at super bantamweight, at a leisure centre in Cheshunt. Afterwards, we managed to talk our way into the dressing room and I saw the belt up close. I thought it was a really big deal and the memory stuck with me.

I got it all wrong in the build-up, however, and had trouble timing my preparation properly. I had filled out by now and probably also thought that by stepping up to middleweight, I had a bit more leeway. But although my training was good, my diet was not, I have to admit. My love of chips would always be my curse.

At the weigh-in, I was two pounds over and had to put on a tracksuit and go out for a run around Ally Pally to try and sweat it off. I must have been out there for an hour running round a park I used to play in when I was a kid. When I came back, I made the weight but you don't want to be doing that the day before a fight.

My performance showed why. I boxed dehydrated and was sluggish. How I got through the 10 rounds - the furthest I had ever been – I will never know. Everything should have been in my favour. By now I was 6ft tall and I had a three-inch height advantage, as well as the longer reach, mine being 73 inches. Also, I was just 24 to his 33 years of age. But my stamina was definitely in question.

In the end the end it was a comfortable win, by a unanimous points decision, but it was anything but a comfortable experience. I was shattered and could hardly move afterwards. The whole episode was a big lesson to me, that I needed to do my weight properly and more professionally next time.

Still, I was delighted to have won the belt and to have achieved something as a professional. It may only have been the Southern Area but I had now won titles as both an amateur and a pro. I'd also earned a few quid, £9,000 basic with commission on the tickets my brother Lee had sold on my behalf taking it into five figures.

Any attempt to be more professional in my preparation went pretty much to waste in my next fight, however. In fact, it was a joke. It was again on a Carl Froch bill at the Ice Arena in Nottingham, with him successfully defending his British and Commonwealth titles against Tony Dodson.

Now I always wanted to be top of the bill, but that is often something entirely different from being the last fight on, which is what happened to me that November night. My opponent, Ojay Abrahams, had arrived late from his home in Hertfordshire, which surprised me as I had made the same journey up the M1 and was there in plenty of time.

He was just a month away from his 42nd birthday and it was obvious he was just taking the fight for the money. If it could be called a fight. It ended after just one round with him retiring with a shoulder injury. It annoyed me – even though I had added another stoppage to my record – and I felt for my fans, who were the only ones left in the place and who would not be getting home until the early hours after the near midnight finish.

It didn't feel as if I had fought so I asked Tony and Mick Hennessy for another fight as soon as possible. It came just two weeks later at the Goresbrook Leisure Centre in Dagenham against Paul Samuels from Newport on another of Mick's Friday night Sky Sports bills.

Though Samuels had had a lay-off of three years, he was going to be a dangerous opponent. He had been Welsh Champion at light middleweight and fought for the British and the IBO version of the world title. I was nervous. He had a reputation as a puncher and it wouldn't have been a surprise among the boxing fraternity if he had beaten me, even though I was the up-and-comer. It was time, though, to take a fight that had an element of risk in it for me.

It was another fight that wouldn't go to the second round, however, but for far different, and very controversial, reasons.

The early exchanges saw us finding our range but then with just over a minute left in the first round, he caught me with a right hand shot and knocked me off balance. I touched down on the canvas with a glove but didn't stay down. As I got up, he threw a big right hander that just missed me so I launched a left hook. It caught him flush and knocked him out. Spark out.

For a while it was worrying as he lay motionless on the canvas. The doctor was quickly in the ring and they got him into the recovery position before putting an oxygen mask over his face. It was a long couple of minutes walking round the ring and I was relieved when he started moving and was then lifted up on to his stool. He would be fine after going to hospital for a check-up.

It didn't end there, unfortunately. He started mouthing off in the press about me hitting him after the referee had said "stop boxing" when I touched the canvas. He reckoned I was late with the punch. But I didn't hear the referee. I was just so caught up in the moment.

And anyway, I thought he was a hypocrite. He had come at me with a shot after I had touched down. I was just responding to him with a counter-punch. It was six of one and half a dozen of the other.

It's a strange feeling when something like that happens in the ring. In real life, I am not an aggressive person by nature unless goaded or provoked. But when the bell goes, when you hit someone, there is that buzz, that split second of excitement. You hit and get hit and you feel in a heightened state of being alive.

When you see the oxygen mask over an opponent's face, your humanity kicks in, though. You catch yourself thinking that he's no longer someone to hurt but a human being. He's got family.

I have done things I regret in the ring, to be honest, like getting in a punch when an opponent is about to 'take a knee', but that is the heat of battle for you when the warrior part of the brain takes over. You have to have the attitude that the bloke opposite is looking to damage you, that he pretty much wants to kill you, and you have to be prepared for it. You are just concentrating at those moments on destroying your opponent, winning the fight. And when you're in that zone, you don't see them as a human being, perhaps with a wife and kids. You can't really afford to.

As with something like getting in a late punch, I have sometimes looked back and felt some guilt about being out of order… but then when you think about it, you are behaving in a ring in a way you wouldn't really dream of in real life. Boxing is about channelling your fighting instincts with skill but sometimes you do what you have to do to get the job done.

The experience was another part of my development and would help in future moments when I needed to control myself while still being aggressive. It just seemed like such a mad fight and aftermath. I have seen Paul down the years since it all and he is a good bloke and we got on well.

At the time, it was about winning and moving on. I had a nice weekend to look forward to. Gary was flying back from Scotland the next morning after fighting up there for Repton and we were both off to a nice dinner show at the Prince Regent Hotel out at Chigwell. There were going to be a lot of mates and good company there, like Tony Sims, who was promoting it, and his mate Bryn Robertson, a businessman he did private training with at the gym.

If I thought that the events around the Samuels fight were a bit mad, though, they were as nothing compared to that which was to follow less than 36 hours later. A madness, and a sadness, would hit us all like a wrecking ball and would change the landscape of mine and my family's life for ever.

II

HARD TIMES, HARD TRADE

In the clearing stands a boxer,
And a fighter by his trade,
And he carries the reminders,
Of every glove that laid him down,
And cut him till he cried out,
In his anger and his shame:
"I am leaving, I am leaving."
But the fighter still remains.

The Boxer
Simon and Garfunkel

8

FAREWELL, MY BROTHER IN ARMS

They call boxing the sweet science. After that icy winter's morning when Gary perished, it became for me the dark science, and not one I wanted to contemplate returning to. And it was strange. Back home from the Luton and Dunstable hospital that Sunday morning in December 2006, the feeling was of emptiness but it was amazing how the house was never empty over the next eight days up until the funeral.

Friends and the extended family would come round and they helped drag us through it all, through all the pain and raw grief. People couldn't do enough for us. I remember some who meant well saying that time would heal, but I just couldn't see it. How do you ever heal from something like this?

Mum would later say that a calmness came over her thanks to her deep religious faith and that she had to make sure she organised the funeral properly and be there for the family. She was amazing. She wrote a little message for Gary and Dad wrote a short biography and had them printed on scrolls tied in ribbons with the green and gold colours of Repton for the congregation.

What Mum wrote was heartfelt and poignant. "Son," was the title and it went on: "I love you Gary with all my heart. How much it hurts me just being apart. I had you, I cared for you and watched you grow with pride, and now fate has torn us apart. But son, I know this is not the end. Because I will be with you once again. Love Mum."

They involved us all in decisions about the funeral, with Daisy and Jessica given the task of deciding what clothes Gary should be cremated in. They thought about a suit. In the end, they chose his favourite jeans. Jessica had just bought him a new pair of trainers for Christmas. They put them on him.

My Uncle Dean introduced Mum to the vicar of St Mary's Church in East Barnet, the Rev Richard Watson, whose son Daniel was our cousin Luke's best friend. Mum connected with him straight away and decided she wanted him to conduct the funeral at his church. It proved to be an inspired choice. Richard would come to be a friend and play a huge role in our lives, even after he became the Sub-Dean at St Albans Cathedral.

The day itself was crazy. Mum and Dad had had 200 of the scrolls printed. More than 700 people turned up, spilling out into the road, unable to get into the church. They had asked for people not to wear black or buy flowers because they didn't want people to go to big expense. Just a single rose, if they wanted. In the end, the church was covered with flowers.

So many people came from the world of boxing – including Frank Bruno and anyone and everyone from Repton – and from the East Barnet Old Grammarians football club, where Gary was a terrific little player. Even at that he stood out as a little No. 10, a skilful ball player, and went through the Barnet youth teams. He was good at everything. I think he could have made a living at that if he'd wanted but he'd just taken to the boxing so quickly and naturally and only played football for fun.

Even just driving the route to the church, people were lining the roads, stopping and bowing their heads. Shops were shut. It showed how much he meant to people and our community. As I saw it all from a car following the coffin, it felt like a consolation that so many people knew, loved and respected him.

There was one weird moment during the service where something was said or happened – I can't even remember now what it was – and Lee and I looked at each other and laughed. I don't even know what it was about. Just nerves, I suppose. Just a moment to ease the pain. And the tension. And the silence. And the loss.

There is nothing, though, to ease the sadness of carrying your younger brother's coffin. It was just horrible, just agonising. What made it worse was seeing my family suffer. My own pain was intense enough but watching your family in so much emotional turmoil was unbearable.

Then it was on to the crematorium. And that was that. A void. We had had the funeral to focus on but now there was nothing to stave off the grieving process that everyone talks about, with its supposed five stages.

I guess the denial stage is pretty much destroyed when you see a coffin and then see it being cremated. The anger would take a lot longer to go, though. As for the bargaining stage, we all felt it, even if we found it hard to talk about things like wondering what if we had done things differently, like if I had stayed with him and insisted he didn't drive up to Leicester.

Next on the list apparently is depression – and I would come to know plenty of that – before acceptance. I couldn't even think about acceptance then. And as for the other stages, I found that I would go in and out of them. It was never cleanly divided just like that. It was messy and random sometimes. And with family around me at different stages of their own grief, there was a mine-field around us all at times.

All of us had our own memories, our little films of him playing in our minds. Mine was not only of a little brother that I loved to bits, but also of a boxing soul-mate, who understood me and what I was going through. Someone I could also watch over.

People often ask me about his faults and defects and of course he could wind me up, as all younger brothers do. But there was no edge or malice to him. We argued, yes, but just brotherly stuff. We would go round the house shaping up to box but the rule was that you never punched in the face. We had been to the same primary and secondary schools and I had always looked out for him. Dad taught us that. We were family, we looked out for each other. Bright and bubbly, Gary could look after himself, though.

He had been to Finchley Boxing Club a couple of times when he was 11 or 12 but when I went to Repton, he came too. I loved, treasured, the times when the two of us would take the tube from High Barnet over to Bethnal Green. Then the walk down Bethnal Green Road, past all the market stalls selling colourful Asian-style clothing, fruit and veg and cheap electrical stuff. We would be excited, wondering what we would hear tonight, what fights and tournaments had been lined up for us.

When I watched him train, I just couldn't help but admire his talent. You hear stories of sibling rivalry and jealousy but I was never envious of him and his ability, just pleased for him and really proud. Any rivalry was just about making each other better. When it was his turn to spar in the Repton ring, people often used to stop and watch him. The place would be a bit quieter as the bags and speedballs went unhit. In a way, Gary helped me by being so good. The expectation was always on him. I went under the radar – the persistent one, the pretty damn good one, but not the special one.

We were like partners in crime. On the way home we would get a bag of chips by the tube station and were often exhausted on the tube home. Sometimes he would fall asleep and I remember him nodding off with his head on the shoulder of the passenger next to him. I was sitting opposite, laughing, watching a bit of dribble slowly seep from the corner of his mouth, seeing the passenger smile.

I remember Gary's first fight, though I wasn't there. It was in May 1999. I was boxing against the Dockers Club of Belfast at the Barbican in Repton's annual dinner show tournament against them and he was in East Ham. How did he get on? How do you think he got on? Dad managed to get to both fights, coming from the East End into the City to tell me that Gary had stopped his opponent in the first round. I won as well, so it was a great night.

We boxed all over the place and against all sorts of clubs, including trips to Belfast for the return against the Dockers, which was always atmospheric, and that one to New York. The team spirit was always amazing. I particularly enjoyed it when we were on the same bill - and I don't think either of us ever lost when we were. Even though we were individuals and bound up in our own fights, we felt like we were in it together. It was a bit like doubles in tennis. I think if he had lost, it would have ruined my night even if I had won my fight.

Not that him losing happened very often. There were all the titles – the England Schools title, the National Association of Boys Club title, then the junior ABA and the junior Olympics and Commonwealth he would go on to win – but probably my proudest moment with him, and for him, came in the final of the Essex Schools championship in February 2003, three days after his 16th birthday.

He was pitted against Bobby Ward of Dagenham at Basildon and it was a contest everybody in boxing in Essex and East London was relishing, as they were the two stand-out fighters in the region. Bobby was the last English boxer to beat Amir Khan, in their amateur days.

It was a massive atmosphere and I was twice as nervous as I ever was for my own fights. It looked like a man against a boy. Bobby, whose younger brother Martin would come to represent Repton and go on to join the Tony Sims stable as a professional, was mature and strong. Gary was still a stripling. I could see the family were concerned too, Dad, Grandad, Uncle Dean and the rest.

We needn't have worried. There had once been a time in a tournament when Gary had been drawn against a bigger fighter and Tony Burns had wanted to pull him out but he just insisted stubbornly – peas in a pod, eh? – on taking the fight. Naturally he won. So it would be now.

In fact, while it was a great fight, it wasn't even close. Gary absolutely took Bobby to school. I still look back on it as one of the highlights of my time as an amateur. And I wasn't even boxing.

How good could he have been? I have often thought about it down the years, wondered what he would have done with his life. It's hard to predict the future in sport and you don't know who would have been around, but I am certain that he would have been the best in Britain and would have been a force to be reckoned with at world level.

Tony Burns told me more than once that he reckoned Gary could have gone on to be Repton's greatest champion, and the coaches and selectors were certainly looking at him for the Great Britain squad for the Beijing Olympics. He would also have made a fabulous pro in my opinion, probably at welter or middleweight.

When he came to Tony Sims's gym after I turned pro to spar with some very good professionals, he never looked outclassed, even at that tender age. In fact, it was often the opposite as he would outclass them. I remember Tony had to stop one spar because Gary was draining the other kid's confidence ahead of a big title fight.

He was also popular, around the boxing club, around the EB-OGS club, and I remember somebody even set up a Gary Barker Appreciation Society Facebook page on which someone posted:

'Remember this awesome man the man that would do nothing less than run to the end of the earth for you if you asked him. The sky has gained an extra star with our loss.

'Let us remember the good times, the fun times, the funnier times, the moments that made Gary who he was… for me that's every time!!

'I miss the curls
the cardigans
the scarves
the stupid skills in footy
the laughter
the friend
the boyfriend
the brother
the son
the ping pong at the BOGS
the darts
the drunkness at O'Neill's
the times in Malia
the Ole Solskjaer, the baby-faced assassin.

RIP MY FRIEND!!! LOVE YOU DEARLY

Now all that talent, all the joy of living of a curly haired kid with a fantastic future, was gone. After the funeral, and once a Christmas that held no festive cheer for any of us was out of the way, I felt I needed to be somewhere out of all the grief and the gloom, though I never wanted to forget Gary. A while before, I had had a tattoo done on my back of a crucifix and two praying hands. Now I had some words added. At the top: In Loving Memory. At the bottom: Brother 1987-2006.

I felt guilty leaving Mum and Dad and the rest of the family that January of 2007, so soon after Gary's death, but I just had to get away. Away from all the memories of Gary so close to home. And definitely away from boxing. I was finished with it and I was hurting like hell.

It was hard on Gemma, I can see that now. In fact at the time I knew I was being selfish but felt I was entitled, to be honest. I told her I wanted to go travelling for a few months and she told me later she thought that would be us finished. As it happened, I wasn't away too long. I couldn't afford it.

I had bought my Mercedes coupe second hand for £10,000 with the money I had made through boxing so far and now I sold it. I just rang up some internet dealer who came round to look at it. The MOT had expired and all he would offer was £5,000. I was annoyed but he had a wedge of cash in a briefcase and I wanted a quick deal. I took the money and ran. To America.

Gary had a good friend called Ali Izziardo who had emigrated with his family to San Diego, so we thought we would go out and see him – me, Lee and Gary's best mate, Daniel Stone. I just booked the flights and off we went. I needed the camaraderie of people who also loved Gary. And I needed a laugh.

I got one on the journey out. As well as the flights, I booked the meals and ordered a Hindu vegetarian one for Dan. He was starving when we got to the States, which is a good place to satisfy your hunger, mind. I certainly did, when it came to gambling and drinking.

After a few days in San Diego, somebody suggested we went to Las Vegas. So we took a road trip and hit the Strip. I for one didn't miss. There were lots of laughs but we cried a lot too. I gambled too much and drank too much. Anything to numb the pain. Within a couple of weeks the £5,000 was gone. I put my bank card into a cash dispenser and it got declined. I had £50 in sterling left in my pocket, just a plane ticket home to keep it company, so that was that.

Except it didn't stop when I got home and got some more money together, doing odd jobs with Dad. For a few mad months, I went out and drank pretty much every day and night. I just couldn't sit at home on my own and I needed to be with mates. Luckily they were always on tap, feeling sorry for me and wanting to help but feeling helpless. I was grateful to them, as I am in retrospect to Gemma, for letting me get on with it, even if we did have some harsh words now and then.

When I came back from a night out, I would play sad CDs and wallow in my grief, weeping until the early hours. I may not have been oblivious to the grief of the other members of my family, but I was certainly wrapped up in my own. I just didn't like showing emotion around them and I didn't know how to console them. They talk about isolation also being a part of the process and I can see that.

I also found out that the trouble with drowning your sorrows is that they learn how to swim. I remember my Nan warning me that the drinking could spiral out of control. I nodded but would not be able to get myself out of this downward descent for a while yet. In fact, to be honest, I probably traded on the death of my brother if anyone questioned my behaviour. It gave me licence, I reckoned, to do what I wanted.

When it came to working with Dad, painting and decorating, we would sometimes end up arguing. He is an easy-going man and very supportive of me in my work, but when it came to his work, the roles were reversed. He is such a perfectionist and while I was a bit like that with my boxing, I couldn't have the same dedication to painting and decorating or the feel for it and his customers that he had. To be honest, I was a useless worker.

I remember one time when I did this one-day job with him, all he asked me to do was paint a bit of skirting behind a fridge. When I pulled the fridge out from the wall, the kitchen lino ripped and he was furious. We had a big argument that ended up with me not getting paid.

By the spring I was floundering, drifting. Probably for all the wrong reasons of looking for some other way of getting money, and from the only thing I reckoned I could do well, I felt the urge to get back into the gym. I went over to see Tony Sims and he welcomed me back. Over a few weeks, I got fitter and got back into a routine that was good for me and stopped me on my self-destructive path, but still I didn't feel right. Still it didn't feel right being around boxing.

Tony had even lined me up with a fight but I knew I was simply going through the motions of training and neither my heart nor head was in it. I just couldn't go through with it and had to pull out, though I hated letting Tony down. In fact, I broke down in the ring one day and Tony told me to forget the boxing for a while.

That, I was sure, would be the end of it but again the nagging feeling of something being missing in my life, that there was something I should be doing, would not let go of me. I went back again after another few weeks and tried once more for a couple of months. But I just couldn't find the motivation to take a professional fight again. I was in despair. I wanted to box again but I couldn't.

It felt like it was definitely over this time but as so often he would be, Tony was great with me. He told me that it was up to me whether I quit or not, but before I made any decision, I should talk to Bryn Richardson, the businessman who had been around Tony's gym for a while doing some training, and who I had got to know and like. I didn't know his amazing story at that time, though, which just went to show that we all have a tale to tell…

9

BRYN

Bryn Robertson, born in East London in 1967, grew up in the council flats of Bethnal Green, near, and knowing, Tony Sims. Like Sims, he acknowledges that his life was informed by the hardness of the East End in the 1970s and 80s.

After leaving school, Bryn trained as a plumber and cites his proudest job as working on the drainage at the British Library. His youth and career were brutally interrupted, however. At the age of 18 came a life-changing moment – and one that has affected his life ever since.

His brother – named Darren, as it happened – was in a pub on the Hackney Road when a fight broke out. Darren, just 17, went to help a friend knocked to the floor but was stopped in his tracks when an older man stabbed him in the back with a carving knife.

"He 'died' instantly," says Bryn. "In fact he 'died' three times that night with the blood stopping circulating to his brain due to lack of oxygen. Staff on A and E at the London Hospital saved him but he was left with a legacy of brain damage, leading to the loss of his co-ordination and sight."

Bryn became carer and provider, along with their stressed mother, enduring all the episodes of Darren's epilepsy, falls and accidents. A leg break and subsequent infection led to Darren undergoing a series of operations for a whole year.

It sent Bryn on a damaging path involving drink and drugs as he bought a pub and nightclub, then had to sell them off to pay debts. He escaped to Tenerife and started businesses, buying warehouses and opening a supermarket, but personally went downhill further. When his daughter Francesca was born in 1995, he knew he had to change.

It would take a few years, however. Still in acute emotional pain, he finally went to see this therapist called Bruce Lloyd on a recommendation. It was a meeting that would start a process that saw him coming to understand his own condition and exploiting his talent to become a wealthy businessman through establishing supermarkets.

But over and beyond all that, he discovered how he was able to empathise with – and help – someone else deeply affected by what had befallen a younger brother…

"I have always loved and cared for my brother, been his Dad sometimes, but what happened to him made me a bitter, twisted and angry man with a lot of shame and pain and blame.

Sometimes you can't think your way through the pain when you are in active addiction. The only answer is to blot it out. I had to find out the bad in me before I could find the good. And when I did, I discovered that I had been living a lie. I discovered that I would rather help you than harm you. I aspired to be a good person.

Most addicts and alcoholics will tell you there is a moment in their lives that triggered them into self-destruction. Behind it is generally the pain and shame that wasn't treated.

I got to Bruce in April 1999 and he told me I had to go to Alcoholics Anonymous meetings to get well, so I started going in the May. Gradually I began to heal and I became a Christian too. Then something happened which changed me.

I went to see a British evangelist called Nicky Gumbel preach. He came up to me afterwards and said to me that God had given him a message for me. It came from Isiah 61 and said: "You will go to the broken hearted." That became my mission and my life.

I had known brokenness and that it was special and that God had sent someone to hold me up. I had once been on my knees at 3am feeling that my life was broken and that God was holding my hand. After that day, he put the right people in my life each day to get me away from the madness.

I met Darren Barker through Tony Sims. An old friend of mine was sharing the Wanstead Rugby Club gym with Tony, who I had known from years back but not seen for a long while, and I used to go there to keep myself fit. After my friend left, Tony took over training me and after a while he told me he was trying to raise money for a new gym at Hainault nearby. At that time, Tony was at the lower end and there is no money in boxing until the big fights later on. It doesn't filter down. It just runs on gifts and sponsorship.

He persuaded me to fight on a fund-raising bill of white collar boxing and I did some sparring with his pros, getting bashed up at times, but it stood me in good stead. York Hall was packed on the night and I won in two rounds. It was my first fight and the other guy had had five unlicensed and 20 amateur bouts. Bruce came to watch.

I kept going to Tony's gym, liking the atmosphere in there. It was family-orientated. I liked watching boxing on the telly but football and Rugby Union were more my interests then. I have always been around boxers, though, and I respect them for the way they work at achieving their dreams. I have the same ethic. I have always liked a fight. I admire the way these guys are so disciplined in their training and eating and for having the guts to get into a ring.

I had known Darren for about a year before his brother Gary died. Darren was very reserved, a good kid. I was at that dinner at the Prince Regent on the night before it happened and Darren introduced me properly to Gary. He had been in to the gym but I hadn't really met him. I thought that night he was a lovely kid.

I missed the funeral. I was working, building supermarkets in Spain, but I thought I would try to do something later. When Darren came back to the gym, I could see the pain in his eyes.

There was a shame that came from losing his younger brother. I lived with guilt and shame all my life because my brother got stabbed and I wasn't there to help him. I understood an older brother's point of view. You are meant to protect them, look after them, and you live with a guilt that you couldn't do anything about it.

I knew how destructive that pain and shame could be and I thought it was up to me to introduce Darren to someone who could help him deal with that. If I can be of help to someone, I believe it is my God-given duty to reach out to the pain. I didn't really know what to say to him. What can you say to a man who has lost his brother? I knew what to do, though. I had Bruce in my armoury and I knew that Bruce could help him.

I took a chance and asked Darren if he would come somewhere with me. He was very receptive. I think it came at the right time, just as the pain had eased off a bit. There is nothing you can do about death, only what is around it. Bruce had done it for me, taken me from pain to acceptance, got me to move on and not destroy myself any more - as I had been doing when I was walking round with all this untreated pain. So I knew he could take Darren from pain to acceptance.

I talked to Tony about it and he was fine. Thankfully Darren was open to it too. Bruce was also open to an initial meeting with Darren to see how it would go. And so I drove Darren over to Bruce's place, introduced them in a quick meeting, and left them to it. I waited outside.

I was just a guide and it was up to Darren what he did with his pain or whether he boxed again. I didn't know what he was going to do and it was none of my business. But I did know that I didn't want him to suffer for years to come. As someone who could have got into sport but for drink and drugs, that would have been a travesty. The tragedy was Gary but the second tragedy would have been Darren.

I knew also there was hope. I believe that the hardest men in the world feel the most too. They feel passionately about their children. They can look tough on the outside but inside they hurt as well. It's the same with celebrities, who are not immune from feelings just because they have money.

Tough people can feel so much more and often can't move on from incidents in their lives. I often believe that the angriest and most violent man is the one who is in the most pain.

I knew Darren was in the best hands. Bruce had plenty of experience and knowledge, insight and intuition. He was a gift and I knew how wonderful he was. ”

10

TALKING THERAPY

I was still raw after Gary's death, though beginning to function again, when Bryn Robertson came up to me one day in the gym and asked if he could talk to me about going to see a counsellor he knew. He said he had checked with Tony and it was OK with him to talk to me about it. Bryn told me about a bloke he reckoned had saved his life called Bruce Lloyd.

My gut reaction was scepticism. I wasn't sure I wanted my head messing with and I didn't want anyone opening up these wounds just when they were starting, but only starting, to close up, even if I knew there would always be scars. But then, I was still in so much emotional pain with it all, struggling to cope with grief, that a big part of me thought I had nothing to lose.

I was also worried about the way I was treating people around me. It was particularly rough on Gemma who saw me at my worst, my angriest sometimes, but who kept faith in me through the tears and any arguments. As for my the family, we were all there for each other but in these early days, it was still difficult to talk about it all in any depth and we all had our moments of upset. That was coupled with wanting to talk about him, to tell stories about him, if not our pain in any detail, because we wanted to remember him, feared we might forget him if we didn't. As if that would ever happen.

I don't think Tony and Bryn believed I would go to see Bruce but one day I found myself in Bryn's car on the way to his consulting room in a house in South London, just near the Oval cricket ground. Perhaps he was taking me over there on the basis that I might not see it through if I didn't have a chaperone. Or, more likely, he wanted to support me. I can't remember what we talked about on the trip over, but it would have been something deep. Bryn was a Christian man and so was I. Whenever we spoke, it was about something meaningful.

We went up the steps to the town house and rang the bell. After a couple of minutes, a friendly, bearded face answered the door. We followed him in and I noticed he had a limp. I would later find out it stemmed from a painful hip that he would have to have replaced in the near future - so we would have plenty to talk about in that department too.

He took us down into a basement room that was carpeted, cosy and warm, lit by soft lamps, with various paintings and sculptures around the place telling their own stories. A bookshelf contained a lot of self-help books. The armchairs were comfortable. On one of them was a scarf with the name of the designer BOSS showing. It was a statement, I would find out, that another presence, one greater than all of us, was in the room and in charge. A higher power.

Bryn sat in for five minutes introducing us and then left. I suddenly felt very alone and uncomfortable and vulnerable but Bruce smiled at me. All it did was make me burst into tears, all the pent-up emotion of the last few months coming out of me. I was embarrassed but he said nothing, just let me have my feelings, before smiling at me again. This time he raised his hands and moved them up and down as if gesturing for me to be peaceful. I remember thinking: 'This geezer's powerful.'

My initial wariness wore off as I realised just what an amazing presence he had, a wise figure who commanded authority without even saying anything. He was benign alright, but I quickly found out that he had a tough side too. That was part of his personality and his approach. And when he spoke, he was like a wizard waving a wand. I just fell under his spell.

There was a bit of verbal sparring but that was probably because I wasn't used to talking about my emotions. But Bruce doesn't pussyfoot around and he told me straight and very early that this might hurt emotionally. It was all about cleaning out my wounds, he said. About dealing with the trauma. I didn't even know I was in trauma.

Gradually I opened up to him, first about how guilty I was feeling about getting therapy when my family were in so much pain and they weren't getting any professional counselling. He helped me understand how we all had our own paths and this was mine. And because we were a Christian family, they were getting a lot of comfort from that, especially Dad, who always told me to put my faith in God. This was my own guilt, just going on in my head.

We talked about Gary and my pain and boxing and how messed up I felt. How lonely it now felt being without my brother and boxing soul mate to share everything with. I told him how we had gone to Repton together and then he had come with me to Tony's gym a lot, so my loss was professional as well as personal.

And I told him I just didn't trust my inner voice any more, just didn't know what to do now for the best, certainly with my boxing career. Or even whether I still had or wanted one.

He took it all in and over the next weeks and months, we worked through so many issues and subjects. I would take the Northern Line to and from the Oval and when I got back to High Barnet, the end of the line, I would sometimes not even have remembered the journey home and would be left sitting there, deep in my own thoughts, until somebody reminded me it was time to get off.

Bruce gave me books to read and one in particular really spoke to me. It was called The Power of Now, written by a guy called Eckhart Tolle. It did what it said on the cover. Reading it helped me stay in the day, the moment, and just get through and make the best of that until things felt different, if not always better. One of my problems was that I was looking at life without Gary way into the future instead of just for today.

Seeing Bruce was a bit like being in The Matrix. In that film, the main character called Neo, played by Keanu Reeves, is offered a red or a blue pill by a guru figure called Morpheus. You take the blue pill and you can forget everything and go back to your old routine with its blissful ignorance. Or you can take the red one that gives you a heightened state of being. Even if it might be more painful at times, you live in reality and you know you are alive again. There was, though, no going back once you had taken that red pill.

I reckoned, working with Bruce, I had now taken it. I had a new awareness. Like Morpheus said:

"You take the blue pill – the story ends, you wake up in your bed and believe whatever you want to believe. You take the red pill – you stay in Wonderland and I show you how deep the rabbit hole goes. Remember: all I'm offering is the truth. Nothing more."

I remember in one session with Bruce, we were talking about the angel and the devil that I always felt were on my shoulders, the conflict in me between achieving things and self-destructing. He asked me about who I would look up to in life, somebody older and wiser. I told him it would be a Grandad figure, and I guess I must have been thinking about my Grandad Rodney and the important role he had played in my life. Bruce suggested that he would be the real me, my gut feeling. When my brain was playing tricks with me, thinking about Grandad would get me back to my core, the wise voice who knows what is right. He was like my Jiminy Cricket, with my conscience being my guide.

It began to work and my mind gradually stopped racing at 100 miles per hour. I came to know what the stupid questions going on in my head were – just self-doubt and negativity assailing me. I came to recognise what was right and what were my true feelings.

The aim was never about getting back in the ring. When I first went to Bruce, I was probably 80-20 for quitting. But without ever telling me whether I should box again or not, Bruce got me to a place of more emotional balance where I was better equipped to make big decisions.

I went back to the gym again and started training. I would see Bryn around the place and would look at him differently now. Having heard more about what happened to him years ago, I could see how he was now handling life. Gary's death still had a powerful grip on me, was still painful, but I could see that Bryn was coping due to his faith and his work with Bruce, and what that had given him and made him, and that encouraged me.

Then Tony asked me out to a training camp in France with some of his other fighters, including Dave Stewart, who was going to fight for a British title, George Hillyard and Daniel Herdman. I thought I would go along and see if I could get back some feeling for the sport. It was in Morzine, a French ski resort, and I remember plenty of running uphill at altitude, which was hard work but which felt good.

We had a nice chalet and we put up a makeshift ring in the car park for some sparring, to go with the work on the pads and the shadow boxing. Normally, I never enjoyed training camps away from home, mainly due to homesickness and to the fact that they were so full-on. There was nowhere to hide, no place of your own to retreat to at the end of a long day's training.

This camp, though, gave me back a bit of appetite. Tony probably hoped it would, though he was still not pushing me. He could see I was in a bit of a better space and getting fitter. He asked me if I fancied a fight.

I had a lot of things to weigh up. It crossed my mind that it might be disrespectful to Gary's memory but I quickly dismissed that. He was like me. He was happy-go-lucky and I knew he wouldn't have minded, would have wanted me to do what was best for me.

But could I do it on my own, without Gary there to support and back me up? It is lonely and hard enough as a boxer in training without all this. I'd never been through it all on my own. Could I adjust? Well, I thought, I still had my Dad and the rest of the family to lean on. I knew they would be there for me, as they always had been.

But did I really want to box again? Did I love the sport enough to do that? I always believed that I was never really born to box, like Gary had been. I always struggled with my weight and with going through the demands of the long lead-in periods to fights. And a voice, that devil voice on the shoulder, kept telling me I had done well enough already. I'd had a top amateur career and I'd given pro boxing a good shot. Why not just leave it at that?

But then the angel's voice, or the spiritual Grandad part of me, was also convincing. What else was I going to do? I always believed I had skills and talents but working with my Dad had made me realise that I was probably never going to be cut out for manual work.

I went to see Bruce for some guidance and perspective. He wondered how I would feel when I was older if I hadn't given it a go. As long as I was all right with not fighting again, that was all right with Bruce. I got to thinking about it and I concluded that probably, yes, I might have regrets.

Bruce made it clear he would support me no matter what my decision and would talk and take me through the next steps. His job, he said, was simply to help me live with trauma, then put me on whatever path was my destiny.

11

BRUCE – 1

Bruce Lloyd was born in Anglesey, North Wales in 1947 and grew up on a farm, the youngest of three children, the son of an undiagnosed alcoholic mother. He describes himself as being a shy and self-conscious child who hated anything outside the limited world of the farm. That included going to school down the road. His simple logic was, he says: "The cows don't go to school so why should I?" and adds: "I was not very clever in a conventional sense, a bit of a loner, and a kid who loved to be in nature on the farm."

Despite that, Bruce got enough O and A levels to get into Bangor University to read agricultural biology. He wanted to be able to contribute to life in the way he had seen the vets coming on to the farm do when he was a boy.

"When they arrived, everything stopped," he recalls. "It was like the Prime Minister was coming. I saw a cow with hypoglycemia on its knees. The vet gave the cow a bottle of medicine and the cow was returned to normal very quickly. It was like the resurrection of Christ. Why wouldn't you want to do that?"

He would later achieve that goal – but in a very different way to how he had imagined, with human beings replacing animals.

Before that, though, there would be a tortuous path that, in retrospect, he would need to go on before he could understand, appreciate and empathise. There would be experiences that would ultimately shape his career path and inform his work with people.

"I knew I was an alcoholic by the time I was 21," he says. "I first went to Alcoholics Anonymous in 1974 but didn't understand it, though I could see there was something in it. It did, however, ruin my drinking."

After completing a PhD in plant physiology, Bruce became a plant breeder near King's Lynn in Norfolk for five years. He married, had a child and somehow held down a job. Alcohol, though, was slowly taking him over and the very fabric of his life began to unravel. He eventually ended up in a treatment centre, Broadway Lodge, in Weston-Super-Mare.

On leaving, he went back to drinking, returned to Broadway Lodge and at the end of his next treatment was told by the staff that they expected him to relapse within three weeks. This time, though, in a halfway house for recovering addicts, he recognised a change in himself.

Indeed, he realised the path he was on was a dead end road and decided he wanted to help people - and sensed he could. After training, and having stayed sober for three years, Bruce took a job at the Charter Clinic in Chelsea in 1981 before setting up on his own in early 1986.

Since then, he has built a huge, though relatively unsung, reputation as a unique counsellor, his methods being more interactive than some therapists who often simply ask: 'How does that feel?' He engages with his clients, challenging and confronting them directly. He describes himself as being "intense about my job."

Bruce rarely leaves his South London consulting room to socialise and has built his clientele through word of mouth. Initially they were alcoholics and addicts, but came to include also those with relationship problems and victims of trauma. They range across the spectrum of humanity from the celebrated and wealthy through those less able to pay, and include survivors of the Hillsborough football disaster of 1989.

"I am still like the child I was who didn't want to leave and go into the outside world," he says. "Who still doesn't want to tell you what's going on. I am ideal for the job I do - strong and silent."

At first he was unsure about working with Darren – "Whenever I am faced with something new, and have to come out of my box, I am reluctant to take it on," he says of his natural, default position – but he sensed an empathy for Darren's plight. For Bruce too had a sibling, a sister, who was – through her own addiction to alcohol and unable to get into recovery from it – all but lost to him.

"I had been seeing Bryn Robertson for several years when he asked me at one of his sessions if I would see this boxer he knew who trained at the gym where he did. He said the man's whole motivation and enthusiasm had gone, due to what had happened to him.

If Bryn had just said that there was this man who had lost his brother in a car accident and asked me if I could see him, I would immediately have said: 'Yes, no problem.' But to me the big thing was that he was a boxer.

That took me into sports psychology, which felt different. I said I would see him to see if we could develop a relationship but I wasn't really sure. But Bryn was persistent and I felt drawn to it. He is one of the most generous men I have ever met and part of his Christianity is to give back. He paid for Darren's therapy and first brought him in to meet me, and sat there for five minutes before leaving us to it.

I was actually out of my comfort zone, even scared initially. I sensed this meant more to Darren than just getting better for himself. This wasn't just repairing his wound as a result of his brother's accident. I knew this was important for his family and that there had in some way got to be a journey that squared it off with Gary. The process, though it was just with Darren there physically, also involved the family and carrying on something. Sometimes you know it is not just the person. There is also a presence in the room too. It was about repairing his wound so that the healing transmitted itself to the rest of the family. This was not just a simple case.

I am an educated man but this was nothing to do with education. Of people who come to me, 40 per cent you know you will work with, 30 per cent are doubtful and 30 per cent you can't work with. You refer them to someone else. It's horses for courses.

You know within two sessions if you will gel and Darren

and I did. I knew I could do something for him, but could I do something for the legacy he was also carrying? Could I help him fulfill it? It could become a burden if we didn't understand it.

Darren struggled to articulate, not because he is inarticulate, but because he couldn't put words to the enormity of the experience he was having. But I could sense a bond between him and me and a chain between him and his family legacy. His pain was palpable. I could see it and he could feel it. It was frustrating early on as it was nearly impossible for him to put into words. He was hardly able to carry the big weight on him and we both struggled.

I could see it all in his eyes but the question was: how was I going to get at it? Some people give it to me and I join up the pieces for them. With Darren, he wasn't putting it out, it was too difficult for him. I try and see the big picture of the jigsaw but I was not even looking at any pieces of the jigsaw.

At first, I had to treat Darren like he was not going to box again and at that point he didn't want to. He was just looking to make sense of what was happening to him, and that was where I came in. I told him no gym, no more boxing. He had to make the choice to go back into the gym based on a healthy decision – if he wanted to complete the legacy - and not based on a traumatic obligation. I knew I would have to address the question of the legacy, at some point, and I couldn't ignore it, but I had to park it initially.

At first it was just verbal and emotional sparring and he couldn't connect with his pain. It was just silences and pauses. It was like he wanted to play the game but didn't know the rules. I think half of his difficulty was being a boxer, which meant that he didn't show any pain. He took the hits. It was what he had learnt. But he had to unlearn it. And he had to learn to throw in the towel on emotional pain and admit that he could endure it the way that physical pain has to be endured.

Darren knew all about sparring and we talked about it in that context. I alluded to Mike Tyson and said that if he told me a lie, I would knock him out. That metaphorically I had a vicious right hook and I would do him.

All I thought about was helping him with his pain. I wasn't going to push him too hard too soon but I knew he would have go a lot deeper if that was to happen and if he was to address the question of the legacy that had inadvertently been laid upon him. If he came back to boxing, that was.

He wanted to work and we made progress, to the point where he was considering getting back into the ring. It came out in little pictures. I then felt I had to go and see Tony Sims to make sure that what I was doing with Darren was dovetailing with his work. That was in about the August after Gary's death.

I was a bit nervous being in someone else's environment. After all, I was out of mine and at first I just watched. But there was a connection with Tony and we gelled. My style is to get close to someone, to look them straight in the eye. I can tell a lot by just looking them in the eye. It's the only place to look.

I asked Tony to tell me whenever I needed to know anything about Darren and that I wouldn't do anything unless he said. He allowed me to be what I needed to be, gave me the space I needed. I am not intrusive and I don't go where I am not invited.

At the time, I didn't know what his destiny was going to be – but I did know that fate had a plan for Darren. ”

12

THE COMEBACK

Yes, I told Tony, get me a fight. I had spoken to Bruce who told me that the pain of Gary's death might always be with me but I still had to live myself. "Why not just see how it goes?" was his simple question, with its implied advice. It was all the more powerful because of its simplicity and showed how important he had become to me.

Tony also played a big part and gave me a new way of looking at Gary's death. He said that I could even do it for Gary. If I was successful, his name could live on through me. He would never be forgotten and people would always be reminded of how good he was, and would have gone on to be. That line appealed to me. I could actually be a living memorial to Gary. My career could be a tribute to Gary.

Bruce taught me to trust my instinct, that it was there for a reason. Just like some of the bad feelings I had. They were there to motivate. I hated having the feeling of guilt, for example, but it was there to tell me that I needed to make a change. Negative emotions could be used positively. I had been in a fog of grief and pain. Now I had some clarity.

Over the years as a boxer, I had got to know my own body and what it could and couldn't take. Now it was about knowing my own mind. It would be a long hard road ahead. But at least I was back on the road.

There was no point in messing about once I had made the

decision. My comeback was arranged for York Hall on October 5th, 2007, 10 months after my last fight – and 10 months after Gary's death. In the run-up to the fight, I needed some sparring and some money and so I took up an offer and headed for Denmark.

It came from Mikkel Kessler, who was then WBA and WBC world super-middleweight champion and was preparing for his big unification fight with Joe Calzaghe. Some would have said that I was being disloyal to a British boxer – and later I would get to know Joe well and we would joke about it – and I suppose later in my career I might have felt guilty about it. At that time, it was something I felt I had to do. There is a great camaraderie and respect around boxing but sometimes you have to be selfish.

I had been out to Denmark once before, early in my career, to spar with Reda Zam Zam in Aarhus when I was a light middleweight and got £500 for it. He was a good guy and I even had dinner with him and his family. Other than that, I didn't enjoy it, though. It was lonely and I was young and immature. There was a McDonald's opposite the hotel and I ate there twice a day.

I have never been a great fan of sparring. It was just something that had to be done. I wanted to take this one, though, as Kessler was a marquee name. And this time in Denmark, I was more prepared. It was in Copenhagen and I was getting £750 for the week plus my food and expenses. And I had company. Dad and his brother, my Uncle Dean, were worried about me, I think. I was grateful to have them along.

Kessler was a tough cookie, as he would later show in two epic fights with Carl Froch, and it was a demanding experience, as you would expect. Still, I reckon I held my own and it gave me a lot of confidence to think I could operate at that high a level. With my own fight just six days away, I did come home early having sustained a badly swollen eye but I had learnt plenty.

The comeback, at a few pounds above the middleweight limit

to give me some latitude, was on Mick Hennessy's bill for Sky on a Friday night that saw Jon Thaxton successfully defend his British Lightweight title against Dave Stewart as the headline fight. I was low on the bill, against Greg Barton, who never stood a chance really.

Now that I was back, I thought I might as well give it a good go and I found that my hunger and desire had returned. In fact, tactically I picked up where I had left off against Paul Samuels and so went for him from the first bell. It was probably a response, too, to the apprehension I felt. Get your retaliation in first, and all that.

It was a just four-rounder and they can be tricky because if you get knocked down, you lose a round 10-8 and then you've got to win the other three. Instead it was me knocking him over and when he was wobbling badly, the referee stopped it after one minute and 40 seconds of the third round to send him home to Southend early.

It was a good night's work. I guess if I had won the lottery or had a good job to go to, I might well never have come back – until Tony told me that I could do this for Gary. Tonight, I had achieved twin goals. I had made £6,000 that I could never see myself making any other way and I had won my first fight on the road to winning a title for my brother.

Within a few days, Tony was coming to me and saying that Mick had another fight for me - and for a title. The vacant Commonwealth Middleweight title. In six weeks time. I told them yes, we should go for it, as I knew I couldn't afford to turn down an opportunity like this. But I had my misgivings.

For a start, I was going straight from a four to a 12-rounder. The progression should always be two rounds at a time. Twelve was the ultimate and I had signed up for a fight that long. Was I going to be fit enough?

My opponent would be Ben Crampton of Australia and though I had home advantage, at York Hall again, he was undefeated, having won 20 fights in a row after drawing his first one. It would be a real step up.

As well as the physical hurdles, I had mental ones to get over as well. I was seeing Bruce plenty at this time and he advised me to trust my instinct. That instinct, I recognised, was to seize the chance. I also consulted my Dad, as I always did when it came to my career.

"Boxing's pretty simple Dal," he said. "If he hits you twice, you've got to hit him three. If he hits you three, you've got to hit him four." His main thing with me was always my defence. "If they can't hit you, they can't win." He would have been a great coach, particularly with the kids at Repton, but he was a family man and couldn't commit to the time.

It occurred to me that I was unbeaten, too, with my record now standing at 15-0, and the only way of finding out if I was going to be good enough was to get in the ring and see. I took the fight, all right.

The money helped, of course it did, and it was the biggest payday of my career so far with my money now going into five figures. I also revelled in being top of a bill for the first time. I had my face on the posters and they went up all over East London, in the cafes, pubs and gyms. I was the headline act at York Hall. That gave me a big lift. It's a lonely sport, both in the gym when you're training and in the ring for the fight itself, so any attention you get is welcome.

When it came to the night, I didn't actually feel as nervous as I expected to be. It was probably a 50-50 fight, could have gone either way, but I had an edge with having most of my family and growing following there, which motivated me even more. Bruce came too, as he would do to all my domestic fights from now on. I just thought, 'Sod it. Go out and do it.'

Crampton was a good opponent with a good jab, but from the first bell I felt I had the edge – and that I had a better jab. I hurt him early on with a body shot and thought I had him. But he was tough. Later in my career I would face another tough Australian, so this would prove to be a good experience for me.

As did the contest itself, with the struggle for me being the distance, as it developed as much into a mental battle with myself as a physical battle with my opponent.

After six rounds, I got a bit down as I thought to myself that I had to do this all over again. But Tony was great with me and after eight rounds, he reminded me that I was now two-thirds of the way through and I only had four more to do. That gave me new impetus for a while. Come the last round, I was in bits but I knew if I survived it – and he was having a good go at trying to knock me out because he was behind on points - I would be the winner.

In fact, it wasn't even close. In my panic to make sure I won, I had thrown nearly 1,000 punches, which is ridiculous. Two of the judges gave me all 12 rounds and the other reckoned I had lost just one.

I was Commonwealth champion. I had been as an amateur and now I was as a professional. I was delighted and very emotional in my interview afterwards with Sky. In fact, I choked up. Now, just a few weeks before the first anniversary of Gary's death, I had a title to dedicate to Gary's memory.

We marked the anniversary with just a quiet family meal that was naturally a subdued affair, sharing a few memories but still unsure about how much to say. It was at odds to an incident that happened that Christmas when brother Lee, sister Daisy, her boyfriend Sean and a couple of mates had a night out in Watford.

It was all pretty low key until some of us decided to get a taxi home. The driver seemed in a funny mood and was driving like a madman. We asked him to slow down but he wouldn't. It triggered some frightening and painful stuff for us. Our brother had lost his life in a car crash and this bloke was driving like this?

We started banging on the windows but still he drove too fast.

When we started shouting at him, he turned the cab round and drove us back to the rank in Watford.

There, we got out and I got into a row with him as we refused to give him any money. I hit him, I have to admit. The police were called and I was bundled off to the station, where I was put in a cell overnight. It was horrible, just a hard bed, a sink and a toilet. A claustrophobic, panicky feeling came over me. The trouble was that even if I had apologised, I knew nothing would happen until the morning.

When the detectives arrived, they put me in an interview room. One of them asked me what I did for a living. Thinking that being a boxer might count against me, I told them I was unemployed. They told me I must have had a good day at the dole office yesterday then, seeing as how I had plenty of cash on me. I was still flush after the Crampton fight, I guess.

They knew I was a boxer though, having clearly Googled my name, and soon they let me go. They told me that the taxi driver had done this before, so I was given the benefit of the doubt. In the end, Grandad came and got me. It would not be the last time that Watford and the police would feature in my life.

My first defence of my Commonwealth title came three months later, again at York Hall, against Steve Bendall of Coventry. I was the favourite this time, which always made me twitchy. He was a good opponent, too, having fought for a European title. He was now 34 but was working his way back up the rankings, having lost his English Middleweight title, and had won his last three fights.

I was locked on to the job, though, and had him down in the first 20 seconds with a solid right counter punch before he could settle. He was quickly up and although he recovered and I played it safe, I was never going to let him off the hook. He was a southpaw, awkward to many right-handers but not to me with my experience, and he had some moments but I was well ahead when I worsened a cut above his right eye in the seventh with a good right shot, after a clash of heads had opened it up, and the referee stopped the fight.

I always remember Bruce being there that night and as I left the ring after doing my interviews, I saw him at ringside and smiled at him.

"How's Grandad?" he said.

"Grandad's fine, yeah," I replied.

All of me was fine, the sensible, wise part as well as the anxious kid full of self-doubt. I had retained my Commonwealth title and gone from worrier to warrior. Issues and problems, and the deep sadness of the loss of Gary, were always going to beset me, and part of my work with Bruce was to accept that and learn to cope rather than expect things to be perfect. But for now I was back on track.

While I could train myself mentally, though, there was little I could do about the injuries that were about to strike a body that was always vulnerable and grew more damaged as I got older and with the more hits I took. I would feel it all the more when I travelled abroad for the first time as a professional to defend my Commonwealth title – though I wasn't expecting the trouble to come from where it did.

13

COMMONWEALTH AND BRITISH CHAMPION…

I was excited when Mick and Tony told me that I was going to make my overseas debut, and in North America too. It was to be the first step in building my name and reputation with the massive TV audience over there. I had a six-month lay-off after the Bendall fight, partly due to the twinges starting in the hips that would go on to give me such trouble, and partly to rest my body after being active for an extended period, so I was more than ready to get going again. Gemma and I had also just moved in together, buying a maisonette in East Barnet, and I had a mortgage to pay now.

The fight was to be at a casino, on the River Cree Resort, near Edmonton in Canada against Larry 'Razor' Sharpe, another awkward southpaw. As an amateur, I had boxed at Edmonton in North London but travelling to Alberta, nearly nine hours flight time away, showed literally just how far I was going with my career.

I trained hard and worked well, flying out 10 days ahead with Tony and Mark Seltzer, his fight night assistant, who always did the jobs that needed doing, like making sure there was enough tape for my hands, that kind of thing. He also counted down the rounds for me during the fight, which I liked.

The big disappointment when I got there was finding out that the fight would not be sanctioned as a Commonwealth title contest because it was on an Indian resort and not on Commonwealth territory. It was agreed then that the contest would be over 10 rounds rather than 12. It was far from the only glitch on the trip, well beyond the twinges I was starting to get in my back. In fact, the fight very nearly didn't take place.

North American rules dictated that on top of the medical, which was fine, I had to have an electro cardiogram test. The doctor took one look at the results and told me I couldn't fight. I had too low a resting heart beat, at 36 beats per minute, and it was skipping a beat, he said. He reckoned I had the heart of a dying nine-year-old. Thanks. That was ridiculous.

I couldn't think what the reason might be. Whether there were abnormalities, as the doctor saw it, was because I hadn't eaten properly - because you don't in the last few days before the weigh-in – or whether I was dehydrated, I don't know. Suddenly I was worried about the fight being called off, having come all this way and worked this hard, and then not getting paid. I was on £15,000, not a fortune but a decent payday for me.

Right up until the early hours of the morning, we were out at various hospitals trying to get another ECG done but none could or would do it at that short notice. My mood wasn't improved on seeing a dead body being wheeled past me while I was in the waiting room at one place.

We got back to the hotel in the middle of the night and I dozed off for a few hours but was then woken at 7am by Tony. Mick Hennessy must have been on the phone all night because it turned out the original doctor was willing to do another ECG if we could get ourselves over to his hospital by 8am. That must have been some negotiation - and an exercise in building bridges. Mick's North American representative Adam Harris had called the doctor a "cocksucker" when he had stopped me boxing the previous day.

The results of this test were fine, thankfully, and the fight was back on. The doctor accepted that my low resting heart rate was just my natural state. It was a relief. The Super Channel TV station would get their top of the bill and I would get my chance to showcase myself to a new audience. And my money.

I went back to the hotel to catch up on some sleep ahead of the fight. That would prove impossible, though. A fire alarm kept going off in the hotel all day and I don't think I got more than an hour's sleep at a time. The problem was, each room had an individual alarm and not even putting tape over it could muffle the noise completely. The thought did cross our minds that it might have been deliberate, to unsettle and tire me, but it would be hard to prove.

I had watched DVDs of Sharpe and while I thought he looked tough and tricky, I always thought I would take him comfortably. After all the shenanigans, though, I started slowly and he caught me with an early body shot that hurt, causing me to lose the first round.

It woke me up, forcing me to get my act together quickly. I boxed my way back into the fight and began to dominate, cutting his eye in the third round and even knocking him over. The three judges all had me winning seven rounds of the 10 rounds and I was glad to get out of there with my unbeaten record intact.

Looking back, it was another good experience for me, even if I couldn't see it at the time. I had learnt about travelling across the Atlantic and being flexible in doing things differently over there, making sure next time I got my own preparations right. And I had also learnt not to get cocky about an opponent just from watching them on tape.

It had all taken a toll, though. My back had worsened and I put it down to all the flying and the problems of making the weight, which was both physically and mentally draining. As it was a non-title fight, I didn't bother too much in the last day or two about the weight so came in half a pound over the 160lbs middleweight limit but it was still a struggle to get to that.

At that time of my career, I was probably still not eating as well as I should and training camps were an ordeal. I would still eat fast food now and again then tell myself that I would not do it for the next fight. I still did, though, and drove myself mad, both in trying to get to the weight and in being angry with myself.

In fact, I would sink into a black hole of depression probably half way through a camp. With five weeks to go I would still be a stone out and that was OK - I was never like, say, Ricky Hatton, who would have to lose up to 40 pounds - but the last half a stone was always a push.

So many times I would think about quitting around these times but going to Bruce still helped, even if I went less less regularly now. He would force me to focus on the day and my real issues and what I wanted from life. Then I would come through the bad patch, could see that the end of a training camp was in sight, and knew it could be done. Boxing was always as much a mental battle for me.

Not that I could ever ignore the physical demands of just getting in the ring. I had been able to shrug off the pain in my hips so far but then came a training camp in Ireland with Carl Froch just ahead of another scheduled defence of my Commonwealth title, against Jason McKay.

The camp was in Castlebar, County Mayo and Carl was preparing for his first world title shot, which would be successful, against Jean Pascal at Nottingham Arena. My fight against McKay was the following week that December of 2008, and Carl and I were working together, both running and sparring.

Now I had always been a good runner, certainly better than Carl, though he was a decent runner himself, and I would usually leave him behind. Not this time. My right hip was hurting like hell and it was really worrying me now. Then, come the sparring, I was struggling.

Now, I always hated sparring with Carl at the best of times, as I do with friends. For a start, he was bigger. With him as well, whenever a bell sounded, he turned into a machine who wanted to rip your head off. It was good for me, I knew, because his toughness and quality rubbed off on me. A lot of my success was down to Carl and I did a lot of 12-rounders with him.

Not this time. After three rounds, I had had enough and told Tony I would do one more. Carl wasn't in on that information and was annoyed after that fourth, as I had given it my best shot and he didn't have a chance to get back at me. He joked that I had 'Judased' him and he would get me back next spar.

Though I went into the McKay fight less than 100 per cent, and was a bit concerned, my hips at this stage were not bad enough to really affect my performance. The Ulsterman was a tough cookie with a good amateur record and the previous year had fought the up-and-coming Andy Lee.

And for the first time, I would be fighting somebody taller than me. It would mean that my best move, which was always to come round an opponent's guard with a left hook and then come down with my right hand, was going to be more difficult against a longer reach.

I was encouraged, though, by the weigh-in, which was held in the shopping centre in Brentwood, ahead of the fight at the International Centre in the Essex town. It was freezing and I thought he looked terrible on the scales – drained and drawn. That told me he had had a worse time making the weight than I had.

As a result I boxed differently. I was aggressive but made him do the work because I knew that if he was forced to throw punches, he would soon tire, due to his condition. I just took the punches on my gloves and could see him growing weary, knowing that I would get stronger.

Eventually his corner retired him on his stoool at the end of the sixth round and I was relieved. While I still had something in the tank, I was growing tired myself, what with taking so many of his punches, even if many weren't landing on my head, and then throwing mine. His face was a mess at the end, with two black eyes, and once the heat of battle was over, I couldn't believe it was me who had done that. You never realise what you are doing to someone at the time.

It was strange. I would see Jason some years later when I was commentating for Sky on a Matthew Macklin fight in Ireland and he came up to me and introduced himself. I was embarrassed that I didn't recognise him as he stood there, a bit heavier these days, with a beer in one hand and a girl on his other arm.

The higher I was going in the rankings, the more time was elapsing between fights. That was partly down to it taking longer to fix up higher-class matches - but there was also an element of not rushing back due to the aches and pains my body was complaining of.

It was in training for my next fight, six months later, against Darren McDermott, that it became clear that the hip problem was just not going to go away. By now I was just jogging rather than running, and not long distances. I was doing nothing to increase my stamina, even if I was still doing the boxing work in the gym on the pads, the heavy bag, the skipping, the cycling and the sparring. The question would not be about my ability, more my staying power.

But I was on a mission. I was doing this for Gary and I had fans, and a good number now, who had bought tickets for the fight at Watford Colosseum. It was probably why I came out with guns blazing on the night. I had also, I have to admit, been riled by some of McDermott's comments before the fight about what he was going to do to me. I thought that was disrespectful as I had the pedigree, even if he had only lost once in 18 fights. It annoyed Tony too, so we both wanted to put them in their place.

McDermott also had a big following down from the West Midlands – his nickname was the Dudley Body Snatcher – and what with my lot, there was an electric atmosphere in what was a tight venue. His crew had a reputation and I knew my fans were not exactly shrinking violets either. I remember warning my brother Lee to be careful.

Through my support for Chelsea, I had become friends with the club's England midfield player Joe Cole, who loved his boxing, and he was at ringside. I felt good as the defending champion but I do remember looking up to see McDermott's fans on the balcony above mine at ground level and thinking that there was potential trouble brewing. They would easily be able to pour drinks down or throw stuff.

The first round was messy as we settled, probably as a result of the animosity between us, and the referee warned us both to clean it up. Other than that, the fight went 100 per cent to plan, with me on the front foot dominating off the jab.

Tony was happy with me early on after the first, and so I was happy. I could trust Tony implicitly. He just got me personally and he was always spot on. If I was not doing well, he would also let me know without panicking me. His words were always constructive.

Then, with 40 seconds left in the fourth, I put together a series of right hands that I could see had hurt him. After then snapping out a jab, I went in with a big right that caught him flush on the chin. It was a beauty. Down he went, and for the first time in his career, amateur or professional. It looked for a while as if he would get up in time but he timed it badly and the referee counted him out.

To be honest, when I played it back on TV, I thought it was a dubious stoppage and that he could have possibly carried on. He did take a movement back, though, and I could see why the referee reacted quickly, with safety in mind. Anyway, I just know I would have been straight back in there and all over him, his face red now underneath his bleached blonde Mohican haircut. He would have been eating right hands and it wouldn't have taken much longer.

I had won my 20th straight fight as a pro and successfully defended my Commonwealth title for the third time. Barry McGuigan, one of the greats, was at ringside for ITV4, with whom Mick Hennessy now had a deal after moving over from Sky, and it was good to hear Barry say that I was getting better every time he saw me and that I was a fantastic prospect.

There was an unsavoury side to it, though, as I had feared there would be. Unusually in boxing, it did indeed kick off between the two sets of fans and it spilled out into the streets around the Colosseum, which was a grand name for the old town hall, and the police had to be called to break it all up. From some of the stories I heard later, their fights sounded better than mine. Everything I heard pointed to Barnet winning two fights that night.

It made me the mandatory challenger for Matthew Macklin's British Middleweight title that he had won by beating Birmingham's Wayne Elcock but Matt was soon relinquishing it to concentrate on winning the European title and establish himself at world level.

It meant that Elcock and I should be contesting it and a match was duly made, for the November in 2009, back at the International Centre in Brentwood. I was excited. The Commonwealth title, which I would again be putting on the line, was great but the British... With all its history and tradition, that was something special and something else.

My training had not gone as well as I had wanted, what with my hip playing me up again and me having to muddle through and run though all the pain to get in the stamina work I knew I needed. I didn't say too much to anyone about my fears or about the aches and pains, partly because I am a bit of a hypochondriac anyway and doubted some of it myself, but also because I didn't want to worry myself or Tony by making too much of a big deal of it.

I was disappointed a few days before the fight when Elcock pulled out, deciding to retire, and Danny 'Boy' Butler from Bristol, who had just turned 22, was drafted in. He had been in training, having fought my old foe Darren McDermott just a couple of weeks before and lost on points over 10 rounds.

My opponent may have been less demanding than before but any notion that the fight might be easier did not enter my mind. The British title was a huge thing to someone like me and as a sportsman, I wanted to take it off the best possible opponent. Elcock had also fought Arthur Abraham for the IBF world title and I wanted to test myself against him to see if I could step up to that level. Besides, I was now the favourite against this new opponent and I preferred the pressure of being a challenger.

Butler was game as anything, brave and determined, but he was inexperienced and, to be honest, I was leagues ahead. He was probably also a bit weary after the McDermott fight.

He came out fighting and might just have shaded the first round but after that I was in control, sending out stiff jabs and following it up with some good right hands. Before the end of the seventh, Butler's corner decided to get the referee to stop it. I was relieved, not only because I was concerned about my stamina the longer the fight went on but also because I had taken delivery of some new boxing boots the day before and they had given me blisters that were killing me.

It may have felt a bit of an anti-climax but I was British champion and it was good to have won a fight live on ITV4. I would later discover that the audience at home had been a very healthy 625,000. I was making a name for myself beyond my immediate supporters.

As a kid, I had posters of the British middleweight champions on my wall, as well as heroes like Joe Calzaghe and Richie Woodhall, and I was proud to be joining them. It was such a traditional title to win, with legendary figures like Terry Downes and Alan Minter, Tony Sibson and Herol Graham, also having won it. Now I would be going down in history myself.

My delight was tempered, though, by the frustration with my fitness and the pain I was in with my hips. I would have to put that to one side for now and just hope I could work through it.

Everyone was saying it was time for me to step up a level now I had the British and Commonwealth titles and to get a world title shot, I was going to have to try and get the European title first. That was held by Matt Macklin, and after the Butler fight, my fans were singing "We want Macklin."

There were certainly some big fights out there for me now, with the press starting to talk about a new golden age for the British middleweight scene to mirror the Nigel Benn-Michael Watson-Chris Eubank era of two decades earlier, what with the likes of me, Macklin and Martin Murray coming through. With Ireland's Andy Lee also around, there were some lucrative fights about and ones that could get me closer to a world title as I moved into the top 10 rankings of the world governing bodies.

Mick Hennessy set about getting me a good payday and a contest that would make me a challenger at the highest level. I just had to try and stay fit physically in my work with Tony, having becoming emotionally healthier through working with Bruce.

14

BRUCE – 2

"Darren is a man who feels very deeply and strongly but his problem initially was that he didn't feel he could articulate due to the intensity of what he was feeling. Making that big connection was the most difficult thing for Darren.

He also had this huge guilt that he was getting help and his family wasn't; that he didn't deserve it. He felt he had to be the strongest one. My response was that if he went ahead, his family would follow him. He would be helping them by showing how he went forward.

Once it clicked with him, he got on a roll and became very good at opening up. At first he didn't want to go back in the ring, then he did for Gary, which was fine, then for his Dad and the family. Later that became a problem, because of the burden on him, and we had to readdress that.

I knew his comeback fight against Greg Barton would be his most important, for therapeutic reasons. It was a huge risk and nerve wracking for me, both going through the process and watching him in the ring. I worried that it might be too soon because the wound had started to heal and another disappointment would have meant it opening up again.

It was a tough decision to have to make and, working with Tony, we had to get it right. Darren was getting better but he needed a win under his belt. A defeat and we could have been back to square one, in therapy terms.

I don't know boxing but I do know when Darren is connected up, when he is working. When I went to see him box – and the Ben Crampton fight for the Commonwealth title springs to mind – I couldn't have told you technically whether he had won or lost a round, but I did know when he was connected and I could tell from his demeanour, from his mental and physical co-ordination, whether he had had a good round. It was about being in the now. And Darren always had a good ability to be in the now when it came to boxing.

The worst times for him were always between bouts. Getting into the ring was stepping into the light for him but the brighter the light, the longer the shadow cast by the training and the build-up.

I would always leave him alone for the three weeks before a fight, as he didn't need me to get him in physical shape to fight and he was in his zone. He would usually come back to me two weeks after a fight when it was time to prepare for the next one. I worked on those bits in the middle.

Part of the black hole he felt he went into during those times was his loneliness. He was used to having his brother around, at home and in the gym, and they had been going on a journey together. After Gary's death, he was on his own.

It wasn't just that it was painful getting back into the ring. It was lonely. And while you can live with that loneliness in the ring, it's the loneliness in life that hurts. There was an inability, not surprisingly, to embrace the finality that he was now on this journey by himself.

It could be a very, very dark and painful place and he would have trouble carrying on at those times. He would get very down and negative, very vulnerable and question his own abilities. He would become frightened and worried that he couldn't carry the expectation.

As he grew stronger and better, he had to change his

motivation as to why he was still fighting because old reasons didn't always work. After Gary and the family, he kept needing new motivations to get him through all the times he wanted to quit. Later it would be about his children and the money to provide for his family. The black holes and getting out of them were also about motivations.

At first, it was always a decision based on empathy about other people and his ability to identify with other people and on his compassion for them. For himself, he would have said, 'I don't want to do this.'

One problem was always getting Darren to change his mind and to be open to new ways of thinking. This was essential, however, because you have to surrender or you hang on to old, damaging thinking. There was a stubbornness about him because his competitive nature - as well as boxing - had taught him to never concede, never give up, never surrender.

Some of that was good and would serve him well. It would get him up off the canvas, for example, and help him set his mind on what he could achieve. But it could also hold him back, emotionally. That was the dichotomy of Darren.

In fact, he was always a mixture of contrasts and conflicts for me and it was a question of getting him to accept this about himself without shame, to acknowledgement his strength as a man and a boxer.

It is summed up by Martin Luther King, in his book The Strength to Love…

"A French philosopher said: 'No man is strong unless he bears within his character antitheses strongly marked.' The strong man holds in himself a living blend of strongly marked opposites. Not ordinarily do men achieve this balance of opposites. The idealists are not usually realistic, and the realists are not usually idealistic. The militant are not generally known to be passive, nor the passive to be militant. Seldom are the humble self-assertive, or the self-assertive humble. But life at its best is a creative synthesis of opposites in fruitful harmony. The philosopher Hegel said that truth is found neither at the thesis or the antithesis, but in an emergent synthesis which reconciles the two."

That was Darren and the task was getting him to discover that synthesis within himself.

For me, the culmination of my work with him was him winning the British title and being back on an even keel, the place he probably would have got to had nothing bad happened.

It is unrealistic to expect therapy to win you gold medals all over the place. What is realistic is that it gets you to a place where you can live your life and be free to make decisions.

It was as if Darren had balanced the books. He could say that he did it, he had fought his way back. Now he could go on if he wanted to without his decisions being dictated by guilt. That was probably more important for me to know at the time than him.

From then on I could let him go. If things ever got bad after that, he knew he could always pick up the phone and come back to the hutch. But he was big enough and strong enough now to be his own person. ”

15

EURO STAR

The step up for me was the European title and Mick got me a fight against a Frenchman, Affif Belghecham, at Alexandra Palace in April 2010. Instead of being elated and eager, I was anxious, though. It was bad news, good news stuff. The bad news was that my aching hips were stopping me doing the distance running and the stamina work. The good news was that I was in a good place in my head and paired with a guy I was expected to beat comfortably, given my technical skills. That was the theory, at least.

The title had become vacant due to the holder Matt Macklin pulling out of a defence through injury and I was happy enough to take the fight, even if I would have preferred a sterner test. When fully fit, that was. A few pundits were saying that my record was padded and I hadn't fought anyone decent yet. I felt ready to show them, in spirit, if not, as it would turn out, in body.

Training should have consisted of a run every morning at 7.30 am around Hainault Forest, near the new gym that Tony had just moved into. It meant me leaving home in Barnet at 6.30 am. I would just be jogging, though, and no longer getting the mileage in. Nearer the fight, we would be doing 12 hill sprints instead of the longer distances, followed by a brutal three minutes on the rowing machine.

I would then go up to some office space above the gym that Tony had rented. Here there were beds for me and others in his stable preparing for fights, like Lee Purdy, Martin Ward and Ryan

Taylor, to sleep for an hour or two.

Then in the afternoons, it would be bag and pad work on Tuesdays and Thursdays and sparring on Mondays, Wednesdays and Fridays. Tony would give us Wednesday mornings off. To the pain in my hips, you could add an increasing tendonitis in my left elbow, which was down to the repetitive movement of throwing jabs.

I was developing into one big injury but still did not want to give in to it. I was convinced I would still be good enough to beat Belghecham comfortably. He was approaching 36 years of age, had lost four of his 23 fights and had not fought any opponents of the calibre I had faced. Having watched footage of him, I actually thought I was going to blitz him.

And I really wanted the title, too. I wanted to emulate my fellow Barnet boxer Spencer Oliver, who had won a European belt at super bantamweight. As well as that, Chelsea weren't doing so well in Europe at the time, so this was my chance to do my bit for the club. By this stage of my career, I liked to wear their club colours of blue and white in the ring.

On top of all that, it was to be at my local venue, Alexandra Palace, a short trip for all my fans again. Lee was in charge of the tickets and between us we sold bundles, around 1,000 as it turned out. The fight, being on a bill being promoted by a coming force in the sport, Eddie Hearn and Matchroom Boxing, was to be on Sky Sports

In fact, because of my support and with Sky needing a backdrop of fans, we were put on last, even though the main event was Audley Harrison v Michael Sprott for the European Heavyweight Championship. It would prove to be one of Audley's best performances and I watched it on a monitor in the dressing room. Trailing Sprott, and with his right shoulder damaged, Audley landed an amazing left hand from out of nowhere in the last round to knock out Michael.

When it was my turn, I was buzzing at the first bell because I wanted it over and done with as soon as possible. I was so much on top that it was embarrassing. I knocked the bloke from pillar to post – really leathered him – for the first six rounds, all of which I won. I thought I would have him out of there at any moment.

But, respect to him, he proved a tougher and more durable opponent than I had given him credit for and he survived the onslaught. I had thrown so many punches trying to see him off, thinking I was going to nail him very soon, that I was shattered half way through the scheduled 12-rounder.

You can never really gauge how fit you are until you get in the ring. I always held back a bit in sparring because I liked to know I had more in the tank on a fight night. But I didn't have this time.

I came back to my corner and told Tony that I was totally exhausted. I thought I might even be gone and he might have to pull me out. But he kept talking to me, kept nursing me through, telling me that if I just kept going, I would win the title because I had built up a big enough lead early on.

It was a feat of endurance, every round an ordeal, but somehow I made it through to the final bell, holding on to my opponent when I needed to, which was never my style. It did at least show me that I could grit out a fight, and I had demonstrated an endurance, resilience and toughness that I didn't know I had. It was something new I could prove to myself and I was at least pleased with that.

When the judges' scorecards came through, I had won 116-112, 116-114 and 118-110. Some thought that was flattering to me but I knew I had won so many rounds early on, and while he had come back, he had never outclassed or overpowered me.

Just how gruelling it had been, and how draining the last round was, was shown by the fact that as soon as I got back to the dressing room, I was really ill. Not to put too fine a point on it, I spewed up my guts in fact. I had never been like that before. I was glad to get home and get to bed to rest my exhausted body. I was never one for going out on the town after fights anyway.

Despite the pain and the problems, it had been worth it. I was now Commonwealth, British and European champion and was very proud of myself. As I left the building that night, I bumped into Audley waiting for his car back to his hotel in Central London. "Not bad for two Repton fighters, eh?" he said. "Two European champions." I smiled. It wasn't bad at all.

Now I was comfortably in the top 10 with all the main boxing governing bodies – WBC, WBA, IBF – and a world title fight could not be too far away. Before that, though, a big juicy carrot was being dangled in front of me in the form of a sizeable purse to face Matt Macklin in his home town of Birmingham in late summer, with him being the mandatory challenger for the European title.

After a couple of weeks' holiday following the Belghecham fight, I came back to the gym and once again my hips were sore. Tony took me and a couple of his other fighters to a training camp in Tenerife and I knew very quickly that I was never going to be able to take this Macklin fight, if indeed it materialised, given the state my body was in. He was a different class and proposition to Belghecham. In fact, I broke down out running one morning early on.

I would start off fine then begin to feel a niggle before coming to a stuttering halt with the pain. It was like there was no oil in the pistons. The hip was grinding in the socket. I was a good runner and no quitter but I just had to. It would later turn out that the cartilage had been worn away and it was just bone on bone. It was brutal.

Tony had just recently found a new sponsor to help him with the costs of his gym in the form of a company called Elite Scaffolding run by a guy called Luke Chandler, who was a friend of our corner man Mark Seltzer. I had hit it off with Luke straight away. He was a boxing nut and a great guy. We would become firm friends and very close in years to come.

He was with us on the training camp and after one depressing day when I had been forced to quit the running because of the pain, I sat down with him and confided in him about it all. In fact, I was in tears and in bits. I told him I would just have to quit if it went on like this. He wondered why I didn't just go to see a specialist and have a hip operation.

The problem was, I could not really afford it. People think you are a millionaire if you a sportsman appearing on TV but I was still struggling. My purse for the Belghecham fight was around £25,000 but I was slow in getting that money from Mick Hennessy. Out of that, I had to pay off some debts incurred when in training, when I wasn't earning anything. I also had to pay my 10 per cent to Tony that he had fully earned. Then there was the tax, so it didn't leave a large sum.

We did, however, have a load of cash from the tickets that Lee had sold and I did keep some of that back against what I was owed but to be honest, I was not great with money at that stage of my career. After the fight and in the following days before I returned to training, I would take mates out and spend more of it than I should.

I guess it came from my Dad and Grandad, who were always generous people, though Gemma would sometimes tell me that I was over generous. I was just so grateful to so many people for supporting me, though, and at the time felt obliged to pay them back. Besides, I enjoyed it. I like to think I am a giver, not a taker.

When we got back to England, Luke said he would pay for me to have an X-Ray and a consultation with a hip surgeon and he found one of the best in the business in Dr Johan Witt in Harley Street. After scans, I feared the worst at the follow-up appointment. I wasn't wrong.

Dr Witt told me I had a hip defect that had been there since birth. Normally, people have round joints, like a light bulb, and they should fit comfortably into the socket. My hip joints were almost square, which was causing the grinding pain and damaging the cartilage. I would probably need both hips corrected at some point but the left hip was the worse, he said. He said he had to pull it out and shave the bone to put an end to that grinding feeling and pain I was enduring. He could do it all very quickly, he said.

Coming out of the consulting room, Luke was buzzing. This was going to save my career, he said. "It's all right for you," I said. "You're not the one who's got to go through it." Unlike him, I was actually gutted. I didn't think it was going to be such a major procedure. I was worried, scared even, and didn't want to go through it.

Also, it was going to cost £7,000 and I still hadn't got the money from Mick yet. As for claiming it on insurance, that was a non-starter. I didn't have any. Try getting that as a professional boxer, especially with my medical history.

This was an area where I thought the British Boxing Board of Control should be doing more, particularly since they take a percentage of your purses. They also take from boxers by sending representatives out to world title fights, with the fighter footing the bill, and I reckon there could be more help for boxers to finance medical problems that need sorting.

My reaction to the news about the operation was downbeat and negative, taking in more soul-searching and questioning of whether I could really go on. A night out with Joe Calzaghe helped. "Don't quit," he told me. "You can be world champion."

"Yeah right," was pretty much my reaction, such was my state of mind, but gradually I got my head around the need for the surgery. I got myself booked in. Luke was going to lend me the money and I would pay it back, which I later did.

It didn't stop me being nervous but the operation went well enough. I also had a bit of an odd experience while in the hospital. As I was coming round from surgery and being wheeled to my room, I could have sworn I saw Amy Winehouse. The following day, I thought I saw her again as I was being wheeled back to my room from my hydrotherapy in the basement pool.

The next thing I knew, there was a knock on my door, which was half open and she was standing there. It was weird. One of our greatest singers, whose Back to Black album I loved, was saying hello to me. She had been here a few days for a procedure of her own and knew the ropes. She told me that the restaurant downstairs was the best place for food so she went down and got me a plate.

She obviously wanted a bit of company and the next day, when my mate Dave Johnstone, the founder of the Chelsea fanzine CFCUK, was visiting me, we had something to eat together in the restaurant. You could get a drink there and she had the odd one. I stuck to orange juice. There was a smoking area outside at the back as well and Dave and I sat and talked to her there. We compared tattoos and she asked me where I had mine done. It was all a bit nutty really.

She was a smashing girl but always seemed like she was somewhere else, or wanted to be. It never felt like she was really present. At one point, she told me about a party going on in Primrose Hill and tried to get us to take her there but it would have been a struggle on my crutches. I was desperately sad and shocked to hear of her death through alcohol poisoning just a year later, in the summer of 2011.

After my operation, I was on crutches afterwards for four weeks, during which time I would make regular trips up to Harley Street for hydrotherapy in the basement pool at the clinic. It was all the exercise I could do and it was frustrating. Often I would grow depressed and angry at my inactivity. I was skint and just wanted to get back earning money. That Macklin fight was looking like my salvation.

But it looked a long way off given the state I was in, physically and now mentally. It was turning out to be a shocking year for me, in fact. Looking back, I should have been going to see Bruce regularly but I hadn't been. He had set me on my path, back into boxing, and I thought I could handle things from here on.

There was some lovely news to dispel some of my gloom. Gemma told me she was pregnant. The baby was to be born in December, which would be a great way to end 2010. Before then, though, there was still plenty that I was going to have to deal with.

16

DOWN AND OUT IN WATFORD

I reckoned I deserved a night out. It was now the height of summer after the miserable spring during which I had had the operation, been on crutches, done only work in a swimming pool and put on more than two stones in the process, approaching my heaviest ever weight of nearly 14 stones. I needed cheering up. It was not going to be a big night out. I was just going with a few mates to watch an England game on a big screen in a pub.

Watford would do, we reckoned. But after that night and the incident with the taxi driver the year after Gary died, and then the aggro between my fans and Darren McDermott's the previous year after our fight at the Colosseum, I should have known better. After tonight, in fact, I would never want to go near the place again.

It was the 2010 World Cup in South Africa and England were playing Slovenia. As a proud patriot, I've always loved watching England play. We settled on a pub in the High Street to view the match and have a few drinks. Nothing silly.

After England had won 1-0, I was feeling hungry. So I left the pub to try and find a food outlet somewhere. Despite some good company and a couple of drinks – and I was nowhere near drunk – I wasn't feeling the night anyway and wanted some time on my own. I went and got myself a Subway and sat down in the precinct to eat it, minding my own business, watching the world go by on a nice June night.

Suddenly at the mouth of an alley off the High Street, I noticed three lads surrounding one on his own. The kid was younger and shorter and certainly did not look the fighting type. In fact, he looked petrified. He had his hands up as if pleading his innocence and begging them to let him go.

I didn't like the look of it, and it disturbed me to see the poor kid in distress, so I took it upon myself to walk over and try to sort it out. I asked them what was going on and before I knew it, the kid they had set upon was hiding, cowering in fact, behind me. The other kids tried to tell me what the dispute was about but I told them that this wasn't right, outnumbering and intimidating someone smaller, no matter what had gone on. They should let him go.

All I got in reply was a barrage of "fuck off" and "piss off". That riled me. Despite being a boxer, I had never seen myself as being a hard man but I never shrank when I encountered injustice, intimidation or bullying. I duly gave them some verbals back. I was now walking properly after the hip operation and not in any pain with it – though I hadn't done any running on it yet – and didn't think about the consequences of anything that might happen should this turn nasty. I was just acting on instinct.

Suddenly I noticed the kid had legged it. I didn't blame him. I probably would have done the same. I also noticed that another half a dozen kids had turned up almost out of nowhere. I was now surrounded as well, with at least a couple of them outside my field of vision.

As I tried to move back into the High Street from the entrance to the alley so that I could be in better view of other people who might be around, one of the kids came at me with a punch, which I looked to fend off. It must have been a diversionary tactic because I then felt something hard hit me on the back of the head. That was about all I remembered of the incident itself before I fell unconscious.

When I woke up in the back of the ambulance, my sister Daisy's boyfriend Sean, who was on the night out with me, was sitting over me. He told me that a few of the lads had come out of the pub when they heard raised voices and a commotion in the street, to find me out for the count on the ground. I had blood streaming from a head wound, apparently, though the paramedics had since stemmed the bleeding. Two witnesses would later say I had been hit over the head with a bottle. On top of that, my hand hurt like hell so I must have landed a punch myself.

Watford General Hospital's Accident and Emergency department was like a war zone, full of domestic incidents and the results of violence. Thankfully, though, I didn't have to wait too long for a nurse to put 10 stitches in my head. I lay on the bed contemplating the various aches and pains I had and found a new one. As I put my tongue on the back of a tooth that I could feel was cracked, it triggered the most excruciating pain I have ever experienced. I was screaming in agony, demanding pain killers from the nurses.

They kept me in overnight and I just had to go straight from A and E to a dentist the following morning for treatment for nerve damage to the tooth. I was grateful to my dentist, Patrick McAnerney, in Muswell Hill for performing root canal work and not charging me for it - having heard that I had done a good deed – as I was having a cash flow problem without any income from boxing at the time.

I soon heard from the police, saying they had caught the blokes responsible for the assault and though I said I did not want to press charges, they said they had enough evidence and were going to do so themselves. The case would go to court. I was grateful for the small mercy that it would be at St Albans, rather than me having to go back to Watford.

While the incident was not my fault nor of my making, I look back and see it a sign that I was losing my way as a professional boxer. Because of my inactivity, I was going out too much with mates as I was easily distracted and figured it was better than staying at home and maybe getting smashed. That was how it was after Gary died and I didn't want to go down that route again.

I still had a big void in my life without him, still felt the pain of his death almost four years on. I guess I was depressed without really acknowledging it and without talking it through with Bruce or my family. I went back into my shell again and found it hard to talk to them properly. I justified my unwillingness to work through it all as being because I was the strong, silent type and because I didn't want to trouble them as they had their own feelings to deal with.

I knew I had to snap out of this downward spiral. And I needed to earn again. Gradually, my left hip began to feel stronger and I was able get back into the gym. Mick made the Macklin fight for me and I knuckled down with Tony. I was excited by such a big contest.

It was on Sky Box Office too, promoted by Frank Warren as part of a seven-fight extravaganza. In fact, it was billed as 'The Magnificent Seven' and also featured Nathan Cleverly, Kell Brook, Michael Jennings, Enzo Maccarinelli, Derek Chisora and Ryan Rhodes.

The venue was to be the LG Arena in Birmingham in the September. The European title would be at stake, but it was a domestic tear-up that the British boxing fans would relish. The winner's next fight would surely be for a world title, while the loser would have to rebuild, his career set back by at least a year.

Now, with the left hip sorted, I was able to reintroduce some running into my training. And I realised, too, how bad the right hip was, with the pain in that reducing my mobility. As the training camp wore on in the August and the sparring became longer and more intense, I could feel that I was just not on my game. I was standing and fighting rather than jabbing and moving.

The operation had fixed a serious problem but now there were others. I had rushed my recovery in my impatience to fight again. Macklin was going to be a hard opponent and I didn't want to be getting into the ring with someone like him when I wasn't at my best. As my body began to let me down again, so my mental state deteriorated too. There were just so many down moods. I grew anxious.

I talked it over with Tony and accepted that I could not risk my body letting me down on the night and me losing my unbeaten record and going backwards in the world rankings. It was tempting to see the fight through for the money - and I was going to get my biggest pay day to date of £50,000 - but it would have been the wrong reason. I would just have to rely on the generosity of those around me for a while longer. Luke Chandler was a godsend as he was covering my expenses.

And so I withdrew a couple of weeks before the fight and vacated my European title. It was a relief, to be honest. Matt was in good shape and would go on to beat my replacement, the Georgian Shalva Jomardashvili, comfortably. It was frustrating to watch, as were other fights that autumn. The middleweight scene in Britain that was becoming so exciting was leaving me behind.

I went through another spell of wanting to pack it all in and it was a bleak autumn, carrying on in to winter. I went over to the gym to talk to Tony about it all. He told me to go home and pray and that God would bring me guidance. It might not be immediate but I would get some guidance. In the meantime, I should just have a good Christmas.

I knew I had to be strong for Gemma as she entered the last stages of her pregnancy, and then when she gave birth, I could not believe quite how much it would change me and my life. In fact, it gave me a new birth.

Scarlett Rose was born on December 17th 2010, just seven days after the fourth anniversary of Gary's death. Gemma had quite a time with the labour and Mum went with her to Chase Farm Hospital in Enfield. Mum was studying to become a midwife's assistant and was the best person for Gemma to have with her.

It was an ordeal for me too, though obviously not as painful a one. When I heard the baby crying, I just burst out crying too. It was just the happiest moment. In fact the whole family was in tears. I do have a sentimental streak that I have inherited.

There was also an element of sadness on my part underlying it all. It hurt that my brother was never going to see his niece, and that my daughter was never going to meet her uncle. It did, though, give the family a lift ahead of Christmas, which was always a difficult time, carrying as it did so many echoes.

Now, I thought, we would always have a birthday to celebrate at Christmas, rather than just a death to mark. I reckoned it needn't always feel a bad time of year and that Gary would have wanted us to rejoice. I was particularly overjoyed to give my Mum and Dad a grandchild as Lee and his girlfriend Enza had with my nephew, young George, and niece Grace. It would be a first grandchild, for Gem's Mum and Dad, Janet and Charlie.

I went out and celebrated – by getting a tattoo on my wrist of a rose with the name of Scarlett around it. It was done by a bloke in Muswell Hill called Lal Hardy whose work I liked. He was busy but slotted me in, given the circumstances. I also had some work done on my back to take in shafts of sunlight and doves to enhance the tattoo for Gary.

People had told me that becoming a Dad would be life-changing and that they couldn't imagine loving anyone like they loved their child, their own flesh and blood. I had been a bit worried, wondering if I would feel the same but I did. Immediately. I felt as if I had done the job I had been put on earth for. It felt for me like producing another person was the ultimate thing in life. A horrendous year was rescued by this wonderful gift.

I began to think also that I was put on this planet to box, too. I had always been a bit selfish, like everyone is in their own way, and liked to go out with my mates without any responsibility. Now I had somebody to take care of and it was time to rethink both my life and my career as a new year arrived. First there was something that needed to be taken care of.

17

TIME TO HEARN

The assault case came to court in the January of 2011 and I went up to St Albans Crown Court with Sean. In the end, I wasn't called as a witness as the three yobs who the police had caught and charged for working me over were pleading guilty and I was told I wasn't needed as it was pretty much an open and shut case. I was glad I wasn't summoned to the box because if I had seen them in the dock, I might have been tempted to run over and chin them.

I read all about it later, though, and how the prosecution lawyer had outlined the series of events which led to me needing more than £1,000 worth of dental work as well as the stitches in my head. He told them that according to some witnesses, I had also been kicked in the head, which I didn't remember as I had blacked out by then from the bottle that caught me across the back of the head.

I was a bit taken aback when I heard the judge's remarks about me – thankfully in a good way. Judge John Plumstead said: "Mr Barker's evening was ruined and he has been left with permanent dental problems because he tried to stop some trouble. He is a brave man. He behaved in a way most of us are not brave enough to do and suffered as a result."

Despite being bang to rights, two of the three who were caught, aged 20 and 22, both from Watford, may have pleaded guilty to affray but they tried to deny being part of the assault on me. It cut no ice. The other one, aged 25, had previous. He was given a 12-month community order on top of the three-month curfew from 9pm to 4am that the others also got.

I suppose I got some justice but to me, the sentences were piffling and sent out no kind of message. This kind of violence was all too prevalent in town centres, with people throwing their weight about. In fact, I was disgusted. At least the judge ordered them to pay me £500 in compensation, which I gave to my dentist, along with a £250 citizen's award the judge ordered to be paid to me.

The Sheriff of Hertfordshire also wanted to give me an award but I didn't want all that fuss and I declined. In all honesty, I didn't want to go through the court case and had it been left to me, I would have found the blokes and sorted it out myself. It might not have been right - legally, anyway - but that's what I would have done.

Once that was out of the way, I reckoned it was time to put the remnants of the last year behind me and make some changes this New Year. I knew I needed to do something different on the basis that if you do what you always did, you get what you always got. That was the sort of thing that Bruce used to say to me in our sessions.

One night, in fact, when Scarlett was crying during the night and Gemma was sorting her out, I got up and went pacing around the place. I then fell asleep on the sofa and had such a vivid dream. When I woke up, I was sweating and could recall the most important bit of the dream. In it, I had seen Gary and he was telling me to sort myself out and get back into the ring.

I rang Tony and told him of my mad dream and that it was time for me to get serious. We both agreed that it was the very guidance from God that he had told me to go home and pray for. And I had done as he advised.

Scarlett had also caused me to re-evaluate my life and career.

Now I had her to consider as well as myself. I owed it to Gemma, too. I now had a family to feed and take care of and I couldn't afford another 2010.

I resolved that it was time to make some changes and go for it. My attitude had certainly changed. Yes, I had all these pains but I reckoned I could fight on through them if I got the right help and treatment. After everything that had dragged me down, I suddenly felt unstoppable and unbeatable.

It was time to work through these injuries and self-doubt and finally fulfill my potential. I had had enough of being the forgotten man of British middleweight boxing.

Luke, my sponsor, was helping me by putting some money in my account each month, but what with all the costs of the baby and the mortgage, I was seriously short of money by now and really needed – and wanted – to be back fighting. I went to see Tony and talked it through.

We had both been having our doubts about Mick Hennessy as a promoter. He was a nice man and a good supporter of mine but it had taken us a while to get paid after the Belghecham fight and we wondered if we had gone as far as we could with him. He seemed to be struggling to get TV dates just now, with Sky not going to renew his contract with them, and I was concerned I might struggle to get the big fights at the big venues.

Tony, meanwhile, had built up a decent stable of boxers at his gym by now and thought he might be able to promote us himself. So he went to see Adam Smith, the Head of Boxing at Sky Sports. Adam said they were dealing with too many promoters already but that they were impressed with Eddie Hearn, who was delivering an exciting new idea called Prizefighter for them. It consisted of taking a weight division, signing up eight boxers then having them box off over three rounds towards a final, all on one night. It was held at York Hall and Sky loved it, as it offered a tournament and contained three hours of terrific entertainment for the boxing fan.

And so Tony called Eddie and we were invited over to Mascalls near Brentwood, the headquarters of Matchroom, the company established by the legendary Barry Hearn, Eddie's Dad. It was quite some place, a mansion with a beautiful indoor swimming pool, where Barry had lived for a while and where Eddie had grown up.

Under Barry, Matchroom were huge in darts and snooker, promoting their world championships among many other tournaments, all with big TV deals. They also then owned Leyton Orient Football Club. Eddie's passion was boxing and he was looking to get into it properly. He had grown up with the sport when his Dad was heavily involved with it in the 1990s, before Barry had fallen out of love with it. Eddie never had, though. He was a real buff and knew all the fighters, all the weights.

I had met Eddie and Barry before, around the Ally Pally show when I fought Belghecham and Eddie was looking after Audley Harrison. Eddie was hosting the press conference a few days before the night itself and I thought he was a sharp operator. I had no thoughts of signing for them then, though. I didn't even know they were looking to sign anyone. From what I understood, Eddie was just doing Audley a favour temporarily and Prizefighter was their main thing.

Now, spending more time with him, I started to like Eddie. He is just such a funny, charismatic character and we were joking around almost immediately. And he was straight with us. He didn't offer us the world but said he would deliver big fights. You could hear the intent in his voice and I felt right away that we would be stepping up a level. Tony and I came away buzzing. Eddie was different class.

Within a few days, he came down to the gym in Hainault with a three-fight contract and I was more than happy to sign it. I was the first fighter he had signed full-time and I suppose there was some risk involved for me, with him still being an inexperienced promoter, but I knew I needed fresh impetus to get out of the rut that I had not only created but also furnished. Eddie's whole persona told me he could be that catalyst for me and he would soon give me the lift I needed.

Eddie quickly made me feel like a star of British boxing. He took me out to a tailor and had two suits made for me, a black and a grey. He took me out for dinner at the expensive Nobu on Park Lane. I had already signed so he didn't have to. And he propelled and projected me. I felt I was on the move.

It was funny. During the dark days of the previous year, when I was strapped for cash, I did some work for Gemma's Dad, who had a removals company. One of the jobs I got sent on was to the Hilton Hotel in Park Lane, delivering new mattresses. It was hard work, getting the old ones out and the new ones in quickly so as not to disturb the guests or the smooth running of the hotel, but I enjoyed it. It was a change from my routine as a boxer.

Now here I was in the West End of London enjoying fine dining next to a place where I had been doing manual work not so long ago. Funny how life can treat you, how you can be taken up and down. The skill was in making the most of all the situations that confronted you, of living in the now. I had come to learn that from Bruce.

Now I was back on the up and soon Eddie was as good as his word about getting me big fights. Another fight with Macklin had been mooted for the European crown but Matt withdrew when he got a world title shot against Felix Sturm, the Bosnian-German, and vacated the European.

Eddie duly got me a comeback contest for the title. It was to be at a top venue as well – Olympia, in Kensington – against the Italian Domenico Spada in the April. I was to get £40,000, which was pretty good, seeing as I hadn't fought for a year.

I still got injuries during the training camp, on top of twinges in my right hip which were fortunately not enough to stop me doing the running. I did, after all, have a new attitude now and was willing to run through the pain. In fact, I could now run seven miles in 50 minutes again, which I was doing four times a week at the start of the camp. There was also hill sprinting twice a week, which Tony had me doing pulling a heavy tyre.

What bothered me more was an elbow injury I sustained during sparring when I missed with a left-handed shot and after that, I was wary of throwing too many jabs. Tony reckoned I needed some treatment and help was at hand – from Chelsea Football Club.

An old schoolfriend, Lee Waite, a soldier who had been in Afghanistan - and a fellow Blues fan – had once given my number, with my permission, to Dave Johnstone from the CFCUK fanzine, so he could do an article on me. Dave – who could always be heard outside Stamford Bridge shouting: "Get your Chelsea fanzine, only a pound. Hurry up!" – became a mate after that and when he heard about my injury, recommended a doctor called Ralph Rogers, who had done some work for Chelsea.

Dr Rogers was a specialist in sports injuries based in Harley Street and he decided I might benefit from blood spinning, a process that the World Anti-Doping Agency had declared was OK just that January.

The process involved taking 10 millilitres of blood out of my right arm, then putting it into a machine that spun 200 times a second, so that it came out with all the plasma at the top and the blood at the bottom. The plasma was then injected into my left elbow and was supposed to speed recovery, though in all honesty, any benefits I may have felt were probably more psychological than physical.

I also had a cortisone injection, which would be one of several I would have over the next few years. They were always prescribed and administered by doctors.

Mentally, I was certainly in a better place than I had been for

FATHER AND SONS... Dad Terry in training at Repton (left) ahead of becoming ABA champion in 1980 and (below) with me and Gary as novices.

GOLDEN BOYS...

Above: Me, Ryan Pickard – who would go on to be Repton club captain – and Gary with head coach Tony Burns on a trip to New York.

Below: Me with Commonwealth Games gold and, right, Gary and Ryan with junior Commonwealth golds.

CARVED IN STONE... Under the Repton memorial to Gary at what is now called The Gary Barker Gymnasium.

BELTING TIMES...

Above: Celebrating with Tony Sims after winning the British Middleweight title, to go with my Commonwealth crown.

Below: Partner Gemma tries on the Lonsdale Belt for size as Dad beams with pride.

MATRIX MAN...
With Bruce Lloyd.

A MESSAGE TO YOU GARY...
Paying our annual tributes on Gary's birthday.

EURO MOODS...

Above: Having beaten Affif Belghecham to win the European title, but down due to a physical struggle of a performance.

Below: Better in winning it for the second time against Domenico Spada.

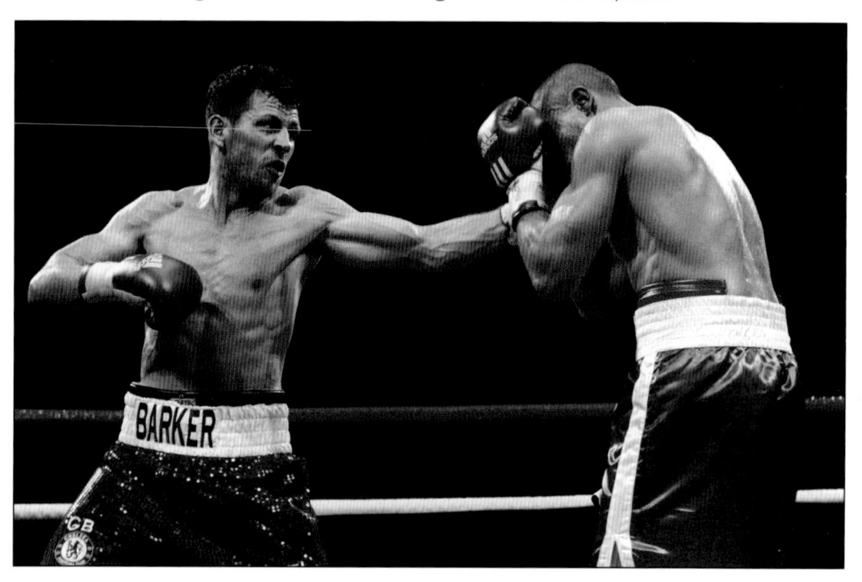

MARTINEZ MEMORIES...

Above: The Barmy Barker Army in Atlantic City, including Mum, Dad, Nan Janet, Gemma's Dad Charlie and Luke Chandler.

Below left: The weigh-in, brother Lee having a laugh as well.

Below right: My trademark Chelsea blue livery.

BOARDWALK EMPIRE...

Above: On the way to the fight against Sergio Martinez, with the entourage of Eddie Hearn, Mark Seltzer, Tony Sims, Luke and Lee.

Below: Relaxed in the dressing room.

FIGHT NIGHT...
Above: Backstage at the Boardwalk Arena.

Below: Martinez was bloodied but not bowed in the end.

THE AFTERMATH...

Above: Lee looks worried and Dad comforts Gemma at the end of the Martinez fight. But I was all right (below), just in need of an ice bag for a swollen face.

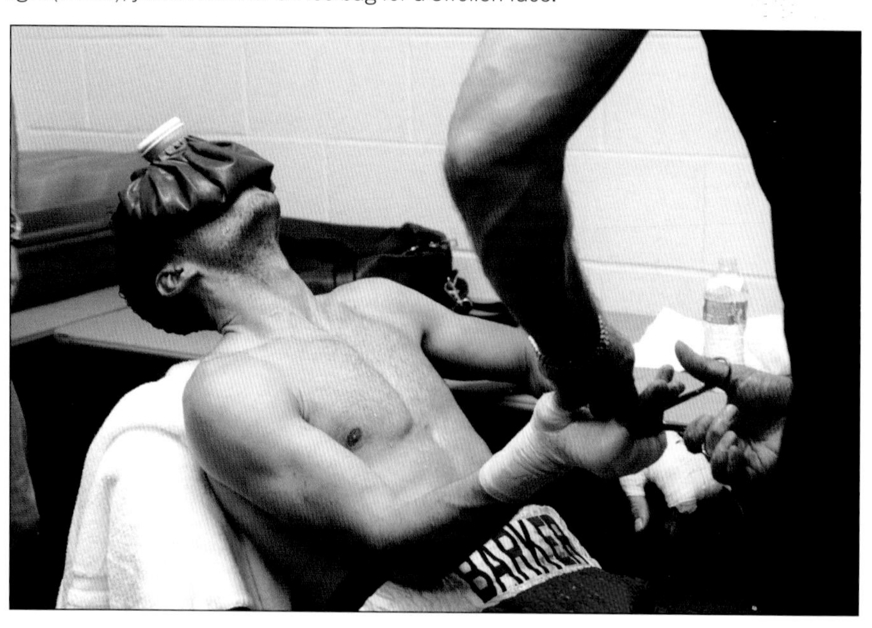

WORKING WITH WAYNE...
In the pool and at a yoga session with fitness trainer Wayne Leal at Chelsea. In the build-up to the Daniel Geale world title fight, it had to replace the running work for me.

OUR GREATEST GLORY... lies not in never falling down, but in rising each time we fall, as a wise man once said.

Above: on top against Geale in Atlantic City.

Below: That career-defining moment in the sixth round.

AND THE NEW...

Down again, but this time (above) at the verdict against Geale. Tony and Peter Sims hug. Eddie Hearn gets a little bit emotional, as do I after being congratulated by the legendary ring announcer, Michael Buffer.

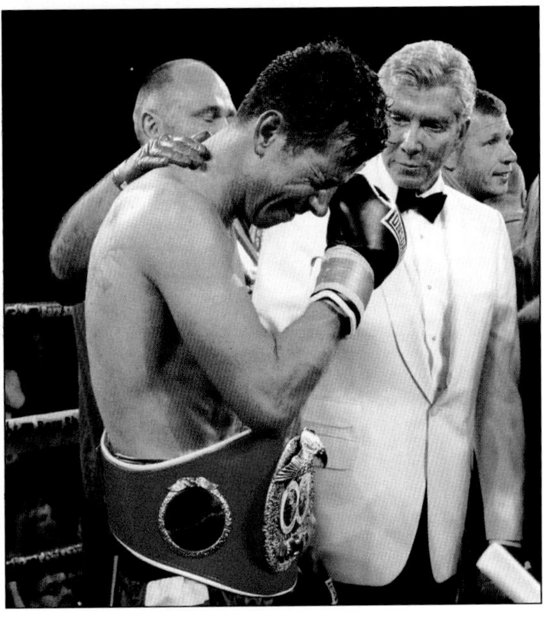

A FAMILY AFFAIR...

Above: With the IBF world title belt and (from left) Grandad Rodney, Lee, Mum, Gemma, Daisy, Nan Janet and Dad.

Below: With the partner in my success, Tony Sims at the press conference.

BEFORE THE STURM...
In the zone for my first title defence, against Felix Sturm, in Germany. But it would be a fight too far, and my last one.

KIDS' STUFF...
Right: Scarlett Rose and the European Championship belt.

Below: Charlie with the IBF world title belt. My Twitter statement sums it up. It was about Gary. And family.

Darren Barker @DarrenBarker82 · Dec 23
It was never about me

RETWEETS 613 FAVORITES 1,465

6:36 PM - 23 Dec 2014 · Details

a long time. Where I had always had that black hole, as I called it, before a fight, usually around the mid-point of a 10-week camp, this time I pulled through without any real depressions. The holes were grey, rather than black. I'm sure it was linked to my feeling physically more confident.

Instead of getting angry with myself if I had a bad spar or session, I would just accept it. As Bruce had taught me, I needed to be more compassionate towards myself and not so judgmental. This time, I wanted to be in the gym, in training for a big fight, and to crack on with what might be left of my career. I was loving being a Dad to Scarlett. I suppose I had some kind of post-natal euphoria.

Come fight night, with Chelsea at home to Tottenham that Saturday, a fair few of my fellow Blues took the 20-minute walk up from Stamford Bridge to Kensington afterwards, in a good mood after a 2-1 win. I had also been on the pitch the week before, at half time of the West Ham game to advertise the fight. Coupled with my Barnet crowd, it meant I had good support for my comeback, after one year and three weeks out of the ring.

I also had good coverage, with the fight being live on Sky, and I knew how much was at stake, that this could even be make or break for me. The Sky pundit Johnny Nelson apparently said that the "whisper on the circuit" was that I was going to lose tonight. I was glad I only heard that afterwards, even though I knew better given the improved shape I was in.

To add to the pressure, I also knew Eddie was losing money on the fight as he had to pay Spada a lot of money to come over. Spada, the mandatory challenger, knew we reckoned him to be a stepping stone for me to get a world title shot as soon as possible so he could hold out for a good price. And I wanted that world title shot quickly as I didn't know how long my career might last, given all these injuries.

Spada, nicknamed the Volcano, was a tough man and a

seasoned pro and I was never going to take the fight lightly given my lay-off. Some pundits were saying ahead of the fight that while they didn't doubt my talent, they were worried about my rustiness as I had not had a warm-up fight. I didn't want one. I wanted to pick up where I had left off and couldn't afford to waste any more time.

In front of a crowd that also included Joe Calzaghe, Kell Brook and George Groves, I was cautious at first and took some body shots. He also caught me with a left hand in the second round. Otherwise I reckoned I was in control, throwing and landing more, and better, shots.

There was a little scare in the third with a clash of heads – his shaved – and my left eye swelled a little but I could see that my punches were also making his eyes swell more, so I was encouraged. I won the fourth and fifth comfortably, seeing one double jab hurt him. I knew I was building up a lead and outclassing him, my three- inch height advantage, and thus longer reach, beginning to tell.

He knew that and began to get in close, spoiling the fight and trying to turn it into a brawl. I began to feel tired and he probably won a couple of rounds, the seventh and eighth. I weathered the storm, however, and by the last couple, I knew I was not going to stop him, as he was durable and resilient, so I just tried to keep my distance and avoid any lucky punch he might dredge up.

In the end, the judges scored the fight 116-113, 116-113 and 115-113 in my favour, which was a bit closer than it should have been. I reckoned I won much more comfortably. Still, I was reasonably pleased with my performance given some inevitable rustiness. I had certainly given a better show than against Belghecham. Tony had told me that my jab would win me the fight and he was right.

The scoring didn't really matter. I had won back the European title and when Dad came into the dressing room afterwards,

I handed it over to him to put in his trophy and memorabilia cabinet. It was another belt to dedicate to Gary's memory, to go with the Commonwealth and British.

Now it was time to turn my attention to the biggest one of the lot. The Spada win had relaunched me back into the top 10 with all the world governing bodies, and as high as No. 3 with the WBC. I needed a world title shot while I was hot again.

I spoke to Eddie and of course Tony, as ever, to see what could be done. Tony had always steered me right, had become so much more than a trainer ever since that fateful day of Gary's death, and in the aftermath he had confided something personal, and tragic, to me.

18

TONY – 2

"After Gary died, Darren was in so much pain for a long time and it was hard for me to get through to him for a while. I just let Bruce get on with it after Bryn had taken Darren over to him and thankfully Darren came back to us. The biggest worry for me was always that not one, but two boxers had died that night.

We were all in bits that day after, we were all ringing each other saying we couldn't believe it, me, my brother Peter, Tony Burns, Tony Burns junior, Mick Hennessy. When I rang Darren, he was crying down the phone. I tried to tell him that I had lost a younger sister. It brought back painful memories for me.

I don't think it registered much with him then but three months later when he came back to the gym, we went for a long walk and I told him about it again and how it happened.

Tina was a beautiful girl, a big supporter of mine when I was boxing. She had a food disorder causing her pain and wearing her out. She was convinced that everything she was eating was making her ill. We discussed it with her doctor, took her to hospitals. Nobody could find anything wrong with her. She had every single test there was. In the end, she was living on lettuce leaves and tomatoes.

Then me and Peter booked her into the Priory for a Monday morning, but the Sunday she booked herself into a hotel and took her own life. Her mind had overtaken her. She was 37.

It was really difficult to cope with. Your own sister. I knew she was suffering but it was hard to know why she would do that.

Darren was taken aback when I told him all that but at that stage, he was still knocked sideways by Gary's death. Anyway, he was 24 then and I was 39. I may have had some experience of tragedy with something in my background that may have helped him but at that time he was still dealing with his own stuff. He was just a kid himself really. There was so much in life he still didn't understand.

He stayed away from the gym for another six months, though we would speak regularly on the phone, and over the years we would talk about what had happened to us both. Like on the training camp to Morzine, in that first year after Gary died when he decided he wanted to fight again. It surprised me, to be honest. If he did come back to boxing, I thought it would be at least two or three years down the line.

Darren was always prone to these down times anyway. On training camps, he used to miss his family badly and sometimes I would find him sitting on his own by the swimming pool just staring into it. He also had a touch of Obsessive Compulsive Disorder, I reckon, and hated change. When I told him we were moving the gym to Hainault from Wanstead, which was a gym mainly for rugby players and was a rat hole, he said he had got to like Wanstead.

But I understood where he was coming from and all the times he said he wanted to give up. After Tina died, I wanted to chuck in the towel myself. Sometimes I would come to the gym and say to myself, 'What am I doing here?' It was the last place I wanted to be, especially if one of my fighters had lost. And I was supposed to be there for them.

Then I would go home some nights with all my hurt and pain and think, 'What the fuck else am I going to do?' I didn't want to go back to running a pub. I could say that to Darren too. What else was he going to do? Like the time when he won the Commonwealth title as a pro and said he reckoned he could now retire happy with himself, having fulfilled a dream.

He was on the exercise bike in the gym when he said it and I told him to come into my office. I showed him a picture on the wall of a boxer and asked him if he recognised him. He didn't.

"His name is Paul Harvey," I said to Darren. "Good fighter. But the reason you don't recognise him is that he was Commonwealth champion. He never went on to win anything higher." I could see it made him think.

I also told him one time when he was down and wanted to pack in to go home and pray to God and He would give him direction. I said to him, 'I am not saying tomorrow but He will in the next few weeks. If He does that and he gives you direction that you shouldn't be doing it, then fair enough.'

He prayed and a few days later he rang me to say that I was not going to believe what had happened. He told me about his dream, about winning a world title for Gary… and he had a totally different tone of voice. I think the Lord spoke to him. When he came back he was a totally different person. Like after his sessions with Bruce. Other fighters in the gym noticed it too. He had gone from being a kid to a man.

Gradually my pain about Tina eased and my faith in God increased... and it happened with Darren too. I was deep into the spirit of God and Jesus and I'd found a church I liked in Brentwood and Darren came with me a few times. I think he knew more where I was coming from then. I showed him pictures of my sister. He knew then that I knew what it was like to lose a younger sibling you had been close to.

At first he never accepted what I said, that with time he would overcome it, that feeling of being so cut up would fade, and he would get on with his life and career. 'I just don't see how I can,' he kept saying. But he did.

Like after that time in Watford when he got beaten up. I said to him: 'What are you doing in Watford at 12 o'clock at night anyway? You are a professional athlete, a European champion. You're supposed to be getting fit.' I could see he was listening.

Moving to work with Eddie Hearn helped a lot. It gave him and me a new lease of life. It was nothing personal. Mick Hennessy had ITV but they pulled the plug on him and he wasn't going to get a new deal on Sky. I was starting to lose a couple of fighters on my books so had to make a decision. It wasn't nice because Mick was a mate.

There would always be ups and downs with Darren but one way or another he managed to get on with his life and his career. And how. I always knew God had something he wanted Darren to do. ”

19

MATCHED WITH THE MARVEL

It may have been the first world title fight made on Twitter. I had just joined the social media site and was interacting with fans. A defence of my European title had been scheduled for July, against an opponent yet to be decided but with Vedran Akrap of Croatia being mooted. I was still angling for an early shot at a world title, though, and I was asked about whether I would take on Sergio Martinez.

Now nobody really wanted to take on the Argentine at the time. His nickname was Maravilla – the Marvel – and he certainly was a marvellous fighter, being undisputed world middleweight champion and well on the way to achieving legendary status. In fact, he was listed amongst the top pound-for-pound fighters in the world at that time - mentioned in the same breath as Floyd Mayweather and Manny Pacquiao - and had just knocked over Paul Williams in two rounds in what was voted the KO of the year in the sport. Having also stopped Sergiy Dzinziruk of Ukraine inside eight rounds, not too many were willing to take him on.

But I most certainly was, and said so on Twitter, tagging Martinez and his manager's Twitter names in the tweet. The next thing I knew, I was getting a call from Eddie Hearn wondering if I genuinely fancied it.

Of course I did, I said. Martinez was a southpaw. I had good experience with them – having grown up learning to move against Dad and Gary, both lefties, around the house and the sparring with others at Repton – and I had good experiences of them.

Eddie had been talking already to Martinez's promoter, Lou Di Bella, and the Twitter exchange had prompted a re-opening of talks. Eddie reckoned there was a deal there to be made. They were struggling to get opponents because Sergio was so good and had latched on to me as a potential match, with a TV date to fill coming up.

Soon after, Eddie was back on the phone to me. How did Saturday October 1st, Boardwalk Hall, Atlantic City, for the WBC title sound? It sounded great. And how did $400,000 sound, around £260,000? It sounded even better. It was more than six times my previous biggest payday after all. Tax of around a third would be deducted at source in America and I would have Tony and some debts to pay but even so, I would be left with enough to move me, Gemma and Scarlett from our small two-bedroom maisonette into a detached bungalow we had our eye on.

My life suddenly got caught up in a whirlwind. Within days, Eddie had whisked me off to New York for a press conference and we flew Virgin Upper Class there and back, staying just one night. This really was elite boxing, something I had always dreamed of being part of. Actually, it was more like the rock and roll lifestyle.

Jet-lagged, we got up really early the next morning and went for a run around Central Park, which was stunning in the early morning summer cool. I felt like I was in a movie. What made it even more fun was the sight of Eddie flagging and unable to speak for a change. I had to leave him behind, gasping for breath. It was just a temporary setback for him. He recovered his voice and would make up for its inactivity at the press conference later.

After one of those fabulous New York breakfasts – this was late July and I could get away with it just for now – we had a look around the shops. Eddie saw a pair of bright green trousers in a window and reckoned I should buy and wear them for a laugh for the presser. It would get me noticed, he said. Get people talking about me. I said no, that I didn't want to be flash.

In the end, I wore black trousers and a black open-necked shirt and though I was trying to look cool, I was sweating buckets for the event, which was at the Rooftop Lounge on Fifth Avenue on a swelteringly hot summer's day in the Big Apple. Eddie and I soon got a surprise and a laugh. Guess what Martinez turned up in? Yes, those same pair of green trousers we had seen in that shop window.

I was clearly an unknown to the American media and they wanted to know all about me. I told them my back story, about Gary, about my amateur career and that I had been used to fighting in hostile, foreign environments. I told them about my professional career and my record of 23 wins and no losses. Then I went for a bit of bravado.

"It's nice to see the New York sun keeping my belt warm," I said.

They didn't seem impressed and I got the feeling they thought I was a nobody, just another bum for Martinez to roll over to keep a TV commitment. The fight was being billed, after all, as 'Noche De Maravilla' – Martinez Night. In fact, I thought I heard a couple of journalists sniggering.

It riled me a bit. "If the favorite always won in sport, it wouldn't be any fun," I said. "I'm here to prove that the underdog can cause a massive upset." And then the words came tumbling out, words that Eddie would later have inscribed on a plaque and put up in the Matchroom office.

"You don't know me," I said. You don't know anything about me. You don't know who I am or what I'm made of. You don't know where I come from or where I'm heading. You know nothing about my highs and lows. You don't know how fast I am or how strong I am or how resilient I am. You don't even know my name. But you will."

There was a bit of a silence and a few people seemed to take notice. I was proud of myself for finding my voice.

I did like Lou Di Bella's comment. Or at least the second part of it. "We believe this will be Maravilla's night," he said. "But there is a man, 'Dazzling' Darren Barker, who wanted this fight. He called for this fight. And you should reward those who want the big fights."

The representative from HBO, the TV company who would be showing the fight live, also said of my attitude: "This is the kind of fighting spirit we are looking for."

After flying back home, I went straight to the Sky Sports studios at Isleworth in West London to appear on their boxing magazine show, Ringside. Then it was into my training camp. And after the glitz, glamour and sheer excitement of New York, I suffered an immediate hangover.

I began to be hit by doubts that I had never had before, now that I was confronted by hard work rather than hoopla. Had my bravado put a pressure on me, to live up to my brave words? You know how boxing is sometimes: a fighter can get led into saying things to help the promotion and to make himself feel good. Whereas when I was in America I had been imagining that if I beat Martinez I would be a superstar, I now began to be assailed by the thought that, though I would give it my best shot, I might have bitten off more than I could chew.

Rather than contemplating that I could be about to realise a dream, I thought more about the money. There had been times when I had been negative before, been apprehensive and nervous, but I'd never been as worried as this.

People like me, sportsmen like me, can beat themselves up sometimes about the fears and doubts they experience. I suppose I imagine that the real greats like Martinez don't go through the same anxieties as the rest of us.

I guess they do, as it is just part of being human. It is probably just that they cope with it better and we don't see in public their fears. It is part of being a boxer, to keep them private anyway.

In the end, after a week or two's training, once I had got back into the routine of the running that I always dreaded, I came through the bad period. I talked to Tony about it. He told me to have faith in myself and my ability. And I did have faith. I remembered a lot of what Bruce had said and taught me about my humanity. About feeling the fear and doing it anyway.

I had plenty to lift and cheer me as well, including my faith in God, and it helped that summer that we were having Scarlett christened at St Mary's in East Barnet, where Gary's funeral had taken place and where we always went now as a family, though I sometimes went with Gemma to her Catholic church in Arnos Grove as well. Two weeks later, I was also baptised and confirmed at St Mary's by the Rev Richard Watson, who had become a family friend and would even come to some of my fights. They were two wonderful days, joyful occasions for all of our family.

My family had always been spiritual and I grew up as a Christian. It was just a part of us and I never had to find God. Religion and my family went hand in hand, and this combination was always there to help me at difficult times during my youth. Dad would often quote passages from the Bible that would relate to how I might be feeling at that time. My Grandad also used to take me to church when I was a kid.

Mum and Dad were particularly comforted after Gary's death by their faith and it helped me too, even if I went my own way and through some bad periods, particularly that first year after Gary died. I was frightened at that time that we might all crack up, though it was most likely to have been me that did. Probably only religion could have held us together.

Looking back, Gary's death never made me question my faith. Nor did it make me ask why someone so young would be taken. It actually strengthened my belief in some spiritual, divine plan that I was not privy to but which required me to act and redouble my efforts to honour Gary and his memory.

While it had always been in my background, and while I had always had a relationship with God and prayed every night, Tony had become a born-again Christian through his own experiences. Our common faith probably explained to a large extent why we hit it off straight away and why we retained such a strong relationship and bond. A few times, we would even go to his Church together near his home in Brentwood. And so I looked to tap in to that faith and I knuckled down to training, my self-doubt under control.

Tony decided that we should break up the routine in the gym at Hainault with a trip up to Sheffield, where the Olympic boxers were preparing for London 2012 at the English Institute of Sport. I may have been fighting for a world title, for which some of them might have envied me, but I certainly envied them fighting before a home crowd at an Olympic Games, which had been the only ambition I had not achieved as an amateur.

We stayed overnight in the boxers' apartments, so I could get in two days of sparring, the most demanding being with Carl Froch, who had now followed me to the Matchroom stable and who would soon be in training for his own world title fight in Atlantic City, against Andre Ward in the December of this year. Carl did a lot of his training in Sheffield, less than an hour up the M1 from his home in Nottingham, because his trainer Rob McCracken was based there with the British team he also oversaw.

The sparring went well and though I could never really say I enjoyed Carl's – shall we say – intensity, he never bashed me up. I was glad to get home not because of that, but because I liked my routine and home comforts when I was in training for a fight. I wasn't the most sociable creature when in the groove, I have to admit.

Otherwise I mostly sparred with southpaws to get used to Martinez. And I preferred people I knew. They understood the job and were not trying to impress. Sometimes, if you get unknowns, they want to have a fight and prove themselves.

While in Sheffield, I had taken on Fred Evans of the GB team and I also sparred back home with Billy Joe Saunders, James DeGale and John Ryder, novice pros but talented southpaws. John was a particularly hard man, as he would prove when we took our training camp to Canada three weeks before the fight itself to get acclimatised to the weather and time zone, Atlantic City being five hours behind the United Kingdom.

Tony had arranged for us to fly in to Toronto then hire a car and drive to Niagara Falls, where we had two neighbouring two-bedroom apartments. With me and Tony were brother Lee, who would do all the cooking, and Mark Seltzer, corner man and driver, who took great delight when we drove through Grimsby, Canada, being a native of Grimsby, up North. Luke Chandler also came out a few days later.

The cost of it all came out of the $25,000 advance against my purse I got when I signed the contract, though I would later have to wire Lou Di Bella for more. The contract also included five return flights to America, hotel rooms in New York and Atlantic City for five people for six days, and expenses for those days of $150 a day for the boxer and $50 for the others.

It turned out to be an enjoyable camp, or as enjoyable as a camp can be in the last few weeks before a fight when you are wound up. This one was especially tense for me as I was going to be fighting in front of millions. I knew inside I could be humiliated and that was always on my mind. What would always make it worse was the decreasing amount of food I was permitted, though Lee's cooking was good.

I trained at Boone's Gym, owned and run by Hank Boone, who we would find out to our shock a few weeks after we were there was killed in a car accident near the gym. One of the reasons we had gone there was because he was renowned as a southpaw coach and was supposed to have a lot of them on his books.

As it happened, they all seemed to be on holiday, though I did spar with one Canadian boxer we brought in, by the name of Steve Rolls. Tony tried to get someone in from America through an agent but the guy they found got stopped at the border on his way to us because the computer showed up that he was wanted for failing to make child maintenance payments.

And so we flew out John Ryder. And this was how hard he was: within hours of getting off the plane at Toronto after an eight-hour flight, he came into the gym and sparred eight rounds with me. He had no concerns about jet lag.

Niagara Falls was like stepping back in time to a British seaside resort with its fairground rides, crazy golf and haunted houses. It was ideal in many ways, providing welcome diversion from the hard graft. I am not sure how moody I would have been without those fun elements. I can get tetchy with people around me but luckily I was with people who knew me intimately and so did not take it to heart. Tony always used to say that I was lucky when I was in my moods before fights because I had him for company. He was the unlucky one as he had me.

Seeing the Falls was spectacular - and on the first morning there, when I went running with Lee, we just had to stop after about 20 minutes to savour the view - but what really impressed me was Lake Niagara and the beautiful houses around it. It was so peaceful and spiritual, the sunny weather helping, and I thought that maybe one day I would like to retire there.

On the very last day there, out on a run, the pain in my right hip returned as we began to climb higher and I had to stop. It worried me, but not unduly this time. The bulk of the work was done now and I had the miles in my legs and the stamina in my body. The only thing that did concern me was if the hip gave out on the night itself but I was banking on the adrenaline to get through.

Anyway, the boredom, hunger and exhaustion were nearly over

and I could see light at the end of the tunnel. I was in the best shape I had been in for years. And despite all the usual scratchiness with people around me, I was in good spirits this time. They had certainly been lifted halfway through our stay in Niagara when we went into a bar on a Saturday night to watch the Floyd Mayweather – Victor Ortiz fight and an ad came on HBO for mine against Martinez for The Ring world title and the WBC diamond belt, which were basically enhanced versions of the world title as they kept showering accolades on Sergio. We cheered and the whole bar joined in. It gave me a real buzz.

The injury twinges apart, everything had gone smoothly. Too smoothly. I knew something would have to go wrong and when the day came, a week ahead of the fight, to fly down to New York for a press conference before driving on to Atlantic City, it duly did.

We left for Buffalo airport in good time but there was a huge queue at the United States border and it took ages to get through. The others were worried they were going to miss a chance to eat the celebrated Buffalo wings at the airport, though they just managed to fit them in before we flew, with me watching enviously. I was more worried we were going to miss the flight. Soon we would all be wishing we had.

It turned out to be a small plane and the turbulence over New York State was shocking. As we were tossed all over the skies, I looked across at Tony and he was reciting verses from the Bible. Luke was groaning, just saying over and over: "What am I doing?" and I felt guilty for dragging him into all this. Lee was just laughing. He had a 'what will be, will be' attitude and I loved him for that. I was scared, I have to admit, but seeing Lee helped.

Thankfully we got down safely and I quickly rediscovered the excitement of New York that I had felt when I came with Eddie for the press conference a few months earlier. Luke and Lee headed straight out on the town when we got there. I went to

Central Park for a few sprints, to keep myself ticking over.

I did my final full session on the Monday at the noted Mendez Gym near Madison Square Garden, and I liked the quote by Muhammad Ali that the gym used – and it was so true:

"The fight is won or lost far away from witnesses - behind the lines, in the gym and out there on the road, long before I dance under those lights."

To be honest, though, the session was a bit embarrassing. Tony had booked it but when we got there, there was hardly a spare bit of space in the place. There must have been four people in the ring working on the pads and all the bags were being pounded.

I told Tony I would just change in a corner by the mirrors and do some shadow boxing and work on the pads with him. I didn't want any fuss. When we got going, some old guy who was obviously a senior figure at the gym came over and asked who we were. Tony told him: this was Darren Barker from England and he is fighting Sergio Martinez for the world middleweight title in Atlantic City on Saturday.

"Yeah?" said the guy. At hearing all that, he cleared the ring for me. Looking back, it was quite funny as the place went quiet but I didn't like all the attention as I climbed into the ring and everyone started watching me as I worked with Tony on the pads. I guess I got used to it as I got absorbed in my training. I was going to be watched by a fair few five days later, after all. I also had a valuable spar with an impressive young southpaw prospect called Juan Rodriguez from New Jersey.

That night, we went out to the famous Gallagher's steak house – mine a pitifully small size in the land of giant slabs of cooked meat and with no potato or vegetables, just a small salad – and we got chatting to the Irish waiter. When he found out I was a boxer, he took us to see a framed picture on the wall of the legendary Max Schmeling, the German world heavyweight champion, who had once had an after-fight party there back in the 1930s. The same painting as in the picture back then was still on the wall these days. The place had a real atmosphere and history.

In midweek, it was on to another steak house in Manhattan, this time Palm's, and this time for a press conference. Eddie was now in town and had joined us. Also at the press conference were Andy Lee and Bryan Vera, whose fight was second on the bill.

There were a few familiar English faces now from the papers, radio and TV, but two months on from my last press conference here, the mood was still the same among the American reporters. Who was this guy and what the hell was he doing in the same ring as this superman Sergio 'Maravilla' Martinez? They may not have put it quite as graphically as that, but that was the gist.

I was glad Eddie was in full voice this time in New York. "Darren Barker is 23 and 0 and he is the British, Commonwealth and European middleweight champion," he said. "He is in the top 10 in every organisation, and Number Three in the WBC, so I don't know what more you have to do to deserve a shot in boxing."

He went on to say that Martinez had not fought anyone of my quality for a while, which upset Sergio's advisor, Sampson Lewkowicz, who wondered "who the hell" Eddie was to be questioning the champion and failing to give him due respect. Sampson cut quite a figure. Around his neck, outside his shirt, he wore a long gold chain with a huge gold boxing glove on the end, resting on his tie.

I certainly respected Sergio but I wasn't going to be cowed either. "I am in the best shape of my life and I have to be because I am facing a great champion," I said. "Everyone says that I look relaxed, not nervous, and I think the reason for that is that there aren't many things I am good at but boxing is one of them.

"This is what I have dedicated my life to since I was 12 years old. When I'm inside the ropes, that's when I'm comfortable. That's when I am in my environment. I respect Sergio but I know that I have what it takes to pull off an upset. I am going to turn the question mark behind my name into an exclamation mark."

I reminded them of the Rocky films that I loved, the ultimate underdog story where a man gets his chance and takes it spectacularly. I wasn't sure they bought it but I think it was as much for my benefit as anyone else's and I was pleased that I had spoken up for myself.

The promoter, Lou Di Bella, summed up the fight pretty well: "Darren Barker has nothing to lose and Sergio has everything to lose," he said. "That makes for a very dangerous fight."

There was definitely more edge to this press conference than there was to the July one, not just in Sampson Lewkowicz's touchiness. Sergio was a man of few words and simply smiled and thanked everyone, but his demeanour spoke volumes, as shown when it came to the photo session, and particularly that picture the photographers like best, of the two fighters nose to nose, eyeballing each other.

At the first press conference at the Rooftop Lounge, Sergio just kept laughing as the photographers snapped away and it triggered me too. It was hard to take it seriously so far away from fight time. But now he looked me straight in the eye, his game face on, and said: "I'm not laughing now." It stuck with me. It was almost chilling, which I'm sure is what he wanted.

That night, I couldn't sleep and got up to walk around the city that never sleeps. I bought a pair of Levis just off Times Square. I felt guilty at eating a packet of M and Ms, worried about my weight. I just wanted some time on my own to contemplate the magnitude of all this and to get my head around it. It was a contemplative couple of hours.

The next day, a limousine drove us down to Atlantic City, about 90 miles down the New Jersey coast, and we settled into our hotel, Bally's, which was enormous. With all its floors of rooms, eateries and its gaming floor, I'm sure there were people who never left it once they got there. It was true about there being no clocks on the gaming floor. The champion and his entourage were in Caesar's

Palace just next door, that bit closer to Boardwalk Hall and the hotel where the weigh-in would be. Now I just wanted this show to be on the road.

I got a huge lift when all my fans and family flew in that Thursday, hordes of them, and it was great to see them all again. It was obviously too difficult for Gemma to bring a 10-month-old Scarlett over, and I might have got distracted, and so she stayed with Gem's Mum, Janet. Gem's Dad Charlie was here too.

Come the weigh-in on the Friday and Barker's Barmy Army took over the Palladium Ballroom at Caesar's, making all the noise, with just the odd Argentinian flag around. I think the promoter Lou Di Bella was glad to see my crowd because, despite our fighting talk at the press conference in New York, he was still getting stick in the American boxing press about this being a mismatch that would not sell tickets and him offering them for free to American war veterans.

As soon as the weigh-in was over – me eight ounces under the 160lb limit and Sergio another eight ounces lighter – I ate a chocolate bar and sent Lee to get me a large milkshake and a portion of fries. I just wanted to eat some filth, I was that hungry. It was nice seeing and re-connecting to people, now including commentators Nick Halling and Jim Watt from Sky.

The worst bit, the dieting, was over. It was funny, in training I always used to like watching that Man versus Food programme on TV but Gem always used to wonder why I put myself through the torture. Now, this evening I could have a big steak but I had to be a bit careful as I did not want to blow up too much and get lethargic for the next day.

After a nice family meal that Friday night, I couldn't sleep again and I liked being awake late the night before anyway as I knew I would still be up this time 24 hours later and I wanted to be prepared. And so I left Gemma in bed to go for a walk. It's a bit of a myth, by the way, about boxers not having sex when in training for a fight – well, for me anyway, though I hear some do refrain – but it's certainly not going to happen the night before a fight.

I walked through the lights and noise of Bally's casino and out on to the famous Boardwalk. It was funny. I had been told that Atlantic City was a bit of a dump but I thought it was a fun place - as long as you stayed away from some of the streets behind the Boardwalk or the far ends of it after dark. It was a bit Blackpool meets Las Vegas.

It was the early hours but it was still busy with the people it exists to serve – gamblers down for weekends or holidays to play cards or the slot machines. Outside the casino floor, it was breezy and the night was getting cold but I walked for an hour or more, enjoying the sea air.

I thought about Gary and honouring his memory, the journey I – we – had been on to get this far. I felt proud of myself and quite relaxed now. Barely a second had passed over the last 10 weeks when I hadn't thought about this fight and now was no exception. I thought about my tactics, how I would start the fight.

I thought, too, about the venue, the great Boardwalk Hall that had seen such legends of the sport as Sugar Ray Leonard and Mike Tyson in its ring. And I recalled my visit there the previous afternoon with Lee and my old mate Waheed Khan, who had come over. I liked to visit an arena when it was empty before I fought there, at least the big ones, to get a feel for my surroundings if I could. I always liked that scene in the first Rocky film where he did before the fight with Apollo Creed.

I contemplated taking on the world's very best in my division, the undisputed champion, and how my life was about to change. By this time tomorrow night, I was either going to be a world champion with glory and millions of dollars in my sights, or I would be reconsidering my future in the sport.

20

BATTLE ON THE BOARDWALK

We met in the bar on the gaming floor at Bally's at 8pm, 1am back home in London, three hours before fight time. There was me, Tony, Eddie Hearn in his slick grey suit, Lee, Mark, Luke and Lee Waite. We headed out on to the Boardwalk and walked the few hundred yards south to the Boardwalk Hall. We looked like the poster for Reservoir Dogs. I felt good, striding along with my hood over my head, getting into my zone - though nerves suddenly welled up in my stomach as it all now became real. It felt good when people recognised me and wished me luck as we passed the bars where people were standing outside having a drink.

I felt ready, certainly physically. I had sparred more than 200 rounds and managed to do the running, despite the ongoing difficulties with my hips. It was a question of believing mentally that I could win. As ever with me, it was a battle between the angel on my right shoulder and the devil on my left. The angel was in the ascendancy just now, thankfully.

The first thing to remember as I walked through the main entrance of the grand art deco, 14,000-capacity Boardwalk Hall, the biggest venue I had fought in, was not to be overawed, either by its size or by the thought of the big names who had fought there besides Leonard and Tyson, among them Evander Holyfield, Roberto Duran, Floyd Mayweather and Julio Cesar Chavez.

And of course Martinez. This was his territory and he was a regular here. The odds were stacked against me. He was 25-1 *ON* with some bookmakers and I was around 10-1 against. Some odds for a two-horse race. But then, no Brit had fought such a pound-for-pound legend since Ricky Hatton with Mayweather and Manny Pacquiao. And Ricky had lost to both of them. I knew that beating Martinez would rank up there with upsets in favour of British fighters like Lloyd Honeyghan beating Don Currie, or Randolph Turpin overcoming Sugar Ray Robinson. And I liked the idea.

I had had a lot of love in the build-up to the fight from well-wishers, including a video from the Chelsea players. It was a real buzz seeing John Terry and Didier Drogba wishing me luck. A lot of the messages came on Twitter but it's funny sometimes how you can focus on the one that maybe shows you a lack of respect. The tweet came from some American fan who reckoned that two Darren Barkers in the same ring wouldn't beat Martinez. I used it as motivation.

I was proud to be fighting the best, because it showed my courage, both physically and emotionally. To have integrity as a boxer, you need to challenge yourself against the best. And for a sport to have integrity, the best have to fight the best. I also thought Martinez would bring out the best in me.

Technically, I thought I was all wrong for him, being just over two inches taller than him and able to jab and move, while he was all right for me. Tony reckoned I was as quick and as powerful in punching as Martinez, with just as good footwork, but what would give me the edge was that I was a bigger and stronger middleweight. We were weighed in also on the morning of the fight and I had come in at 12 stones, after the meal of the previous night.

I had all this experience of southpaws as well, having grown up with them in my family and at Repton. The tactic was to get your lead foot on the outside of their lead foot, jab over their right hand – or throw a left hook – and then follow it up with a right hand of your own. It was my favourite combination.

Tony also thought Martinez might be past his best and ready, at

36, for me to push him just over the hill. His camp was also talking about looking beyond me, to mega money potential fights at super welterweight (the American term; I prefer light middleweight) against Mayweather and Pacquiao, meaning that he might not be as focused on the task at hand as I was, this being everything to me.

With all those kind of thoughts echoing in my head, we walked to my dressing room. I am very fussy about my changing space but I liked this one, down at the bottom of a long, snaking corridor in the bowels of the arena. It was big and airy, with whitewashed walls. When we got there, Lee taped up a Union Jack on the wall and hung up my spangly gown and shorts in Chelsea blue.

On the gown I had the words and numbers: Psalm 21:1. It read in the Bible: 'The Lord is my light and my salvation; whom shall I fear? The Lord is the strength of my life; of whom shall I be afraid?' On the shorts I had my usual words: "In memory of our champion, Gary Barker."

I checked out the shower and set down my bath bag with Scarlett's face imprinted on it. Then I lay on the physio's table to meditate, to get myself in the zone, as Lee put all our music on his docking station. I could feel a calmness come over me, in contrast to the figure whose nerves had increased with each step of the walk along the Boardwalk to the venue.

Family were allowed into the dressing room and Dad, Grandad and Uncle Dean came in. Though in Atlantic City, Mum stayed away, as she had always done ever since watching me fight at the Commonwealth Games, and was kept company by my Nan Janet, Dad's Mum.

Daisy would come to fights and phone Mum afterwards to let her know I was OK and she might watch it later on TV. I guess it must be tough watching your son get hit. In fact, it's a hard sport for family to watch, knowing that the object is for somebody to try to hurt a loved one in front of your eyes without you intervening.

Tonight, Dad and Grandad were more nervous than I was but

calmed down when they saw how at ease I seemed. Dad just told me to stay safe and left all the tactics to Tony. All Dad said on that front was: "Do the business, Dal."

Just before it was time to go out, after I had done my shadow boxing and hitting of the pads, I had a moment with Tony. He reminded me how far I had come. He wanted me to realise how good I was, how good he knew I was.

"You're world class," he said. "I've known it for years. Now is the time for you to show it. You're ready. You've prepared for this for 14 weeks."

Eddie chipped in then. "Make that 17 years," he said. He was right. I had come from smoky working men's clubs around London as a boy amateur to one of the great boxing venues. And I was live on television in America and Great Britain.

The formalities were completed. The referee, Eddie Cotton, came in for his talk, just reminding me about fighting fair. My gloves were taped up under the watchful eye of one of Martinez's representatives for him to see there was no funny business going on. Mark Seltzer went as my rep to Sergio's dressing room.

Then the TV floor manager from the HBO network told us it was time to go on. She led us out to the back of the arena and we waited for a while until my entrance was announced.

My music was cued up and the curtain parted. Luke had played the track to me once in the car and reckoned it would be good for my ring walk. It was. We picked Nicky Minaj's Moment 4 Life because I knew that I would, and wanted to, remember this moment for the rest of my life, win or lose. It went...

I fly with the stars in the skies,
I am no longer trying to survive,
I believe that life is a prize...

I wanted to savour every moment of my 50-yard walk to the

ring. I had watched so many big fights from America and knew how glitzy they looked, just different from ours back home, more showbizzy.

In this very moment I slay Goliath with a sling,
In this very moment I bring, put it on everything,
That I will retire with the ring,
And I will retire with the crown, yes…

I imagined all the people back home watching this, Tony Burns at Repton and all the guys there, even if it was now 4 am on Sunday morning in England.

We done did everything they could think of,
Greatness is what we on the brink of…

I could just about hear all my fans chanting for me - and we were told that more than 300 had made the trip - from their position high up in the seats. Their noise was intermingled with boos from Martinez's fans, along with Nicky Minaj and her chorus...

I wish that I could have this moment
For life, for life, for life,
'Cause in this moment I just feel so
Alive, alive, alive…

And then I was in the ring, prowling, desperate for the fight to get started, glad to be in the place where I performed best and rose to the occasion. Where I was in control. I did what I always did: I went to the ropes on all four sides and bounced my back against them, getting a feel for my area, my space. My workplace. The ring was always the same size, no matter where you fought, big arena or small hall.

I swear, damn, this one for the books,
Man, I swear this shit is as fun as it looks…

Then it was Sergio's turn. The place erupted, with more than just Argentinians waving their light blue striped flags with that face of the sun on it. Martinez had a home in Madrid but also spent a lot of time in California and he had a big American following.

With both boxers in the ring, the announcer, the legendary Michael Buffer – that smart, silver-haired figure whose powerful voice can be heard at all the big world title fights - then announced me and my fight record to the crowd. Or announced a boxer called Darren Baker. He had got my name wrong. It was out of character and it annoyed me. I looked at Eddie and rolled my eyes. I was going to try and use it as further motivation.

Now I just wanted the opening bell, because the nerves vanish as soon as that sounds. Then your head is just in the moment and your body follows. Tony gave me one last reminder of the game plan: frustrate the life out of him. And I knew I could do that with my boxing ability. Let's just get this on now.

When that bell sounds, too, all the talk flies out of the window along with all the bravado. Things said at press conferences, so important at the time as part of the process of building yourself up, beyond the selling of tickets, are forgotten. It becomes just you and him, raw and naked in the spotlight.

I found out instantly and at first hand why he was rated so highly. He liked to crouch and keep his hands low, bringing up punches from unusual angles. They were spiteful, though thankfully without being concussive. He was slippery, too, when you tried to land a punch yourself, his reflexes were slick and head movement quick.

Still, I did well, I thought, in the early rounds. I protected my chin and jabbed sharply, getting my shots away over his jab and forcing him on to the back foot. In the third and fourth I caught him with a couple of right hands. I even drew blood, cutting his forehead. By the sixth, I had broken his nose – yes, broken the great Sergio Martinez's nose – following up a shot that caught him on the button in the fourth. I'd had my nose broken once when young at Repton and knew it was busted from how badly it was bleeding. It was as if a tap of blood had been turned on.

Peering across at Sergio between rounds whilst Tony talked to me, I could see his seconds pushing cotton wool up his nostrils to stem the flow. Seeing blood on your opponent always drives you on, gives you a lift.

Tony was keeping it simple, telling me I was doing well and to keep jabbing and moving, to keep scoring. I would find out later when I came to watch the fight back that Jim Watt, at ringside for Sky, had me ahead on points at the midway stage. The upset was on. I was thinking at the time it was time to turn the screw, as Tony and I had planned.

I tried to. I really tried. But Martinez began to show why he was such a great champion and began to profit from my inexperience at this the highest level. I was so involved in the fight that I was just, well, consumed by simply boxing while he was capable of standing back to see what was needed to win the fight. He saw the bigger picture.

And he was very canny. Take the last 30 seconds of rounds. Then, he would up his game and work rate, launching a flurry of shots to leave a lasting impression in the judges' minds so that he might get the 10 points. That was ringcraft from a fighter of the highest quality and a real lesson for me. Looking back, it was probably also a compliment to me. I reckon he knew that he was in the fight of his life. In the eighth, for example, I got him with a decent four-punch combination but he ended up winning it.

When it got to the ninth and 10th rounds, I knew he was now on top and that I was probably losing the fight on points. I had to cling on in the 10th and he caught me near the end with a right hook that wobbled me momentarily but the doctor who came to my corner at the end of the round was quickly reassured that I could continue.

Mind you, the doc wasn't feeling what I was feeling. The legacy of that punch in the 10th hit home now as I sat on my stool. A horrific shooting pain went through my left ear. I didn't know what it was until it later dawned on me. I had had a perforated eardrum before but not like this. This was like someone had shot me. Or someone had put a plunger on my ear. That multiplied by 1,000. Walking back to my corner at the end of the round, I just felt weird, unsteady, unable to balance. Like Bambi on ice.

Amid the pain and the noise, I heard Tony urge me on. "Do it for your brother, Daz," he said. I wanted to. I really wanted to. But in boxing you need a good base, a solid stance, if you are going to land punches and avoid them in return. I didn't have it. My legs were wobbling. In that state, you are going to be vulnerable, especially when you are trying to land a knockout punch of your own.

And I knew that was probably what I needed to do now, with two rounds left and him likely to be at least three rounds ahead on points. Before I could land one, though, he got me with one of his own. A big right hand disorientated me more – and later Martinez would say that his plan had been to get me watching the dangerous left hand before catching me late on with an unexpected right. He quickly followed it up with another chopping punch behind my ear. I was out of it now. I tried to get up but my legs betrayed me. Eddie Cotton would let me fight on no longer. Tony was in the ring in an instant to come to my aid.

At least, I told myself when my senses returned, I had been on my feet when the fight ended, one minute and 29 seconds into the 11th. I had been just four and a half minutes away from taking the best in the world the full distance.

You could see how much it meant to Martinez by how loud and long he celebrated. He knew he had been in a contest that none of the American boxing fraternity expected. Now people knew my name. Now they knew I was not just some bum lined up as a fall guy in a mismatch.

Later I discovered that the Mexican judge Alejandro Rochin had scored it, when it ended, as nine rounds to Martinez and one to me, but Sergio would dismiss that as being too harsh. He said it was much closer, an even fight, and reckoned he was ahead by two rounds. The two other cards reflected that: 97-94 on Scotsman Victor Loughlin's and 96-94 on New Jersey's Lynne Carter. Sergio also acknowledged that it had been a good punch of mine that had so damaged his nose.

I couldn't wait to get back to the dressing room, not least because I had this strange curiosity about what he had done to me and how it had ended. I went to look at myself in the mirror. I checked my ear. It still hurt like hell though there was nothing to show outwardly that my eardrum was perforated. I saw my bloodied face and blackened, swollen eyes and nose and didn't like it. I didn't want Scarlett to see me like this. I have memories as a toddler seeing my Dad marked after a fight and of it really upsetting me.

The New Jersey State Athletic Control Board doctor was quick to come into the dressing room to check on me and thankfully pronounced no lasting damage. Since it had been a technical knockout, he said, I would have to serve a suspension from boxing of 60 days.

I managed a joke. "Can't you make it longer?" I asked.

Soon all my family were in the dressing room and it was great comfort to see them, even if Gemma in particular was upset to see me in this state. It meant a lot hearing my Dad telling me that he was proud of me. Show me the son who doesn't want to make his Dad proud…

I was surprised when I finally got showered and changed and walked out through the front of the hall to the Boardwalk past

1 am that there were still fans out there wanting my autograph. One lady, in a broad New York accent, shouted to me: "Be proud, Darren Barker. You fought with your heart." It stuck with me. It meant a lot.

We walked back to Bally's, this time Reservoir Dogs with our tails between our legs, and found a bar inside to have a beer with about a dozen of my family and close friends, a number that grew quickly with mates appearing when they found out I was there. I felt moved to get up on a stool in front of them all to thank them for coming all this way, paying all this money, to come and support me. I had a real lump in my throat.

It was funny and it made me smile... when I got there, I was wearing sunglasses and the barman asked to see some ID but someone bought me a beer. I was 29 now and I certainly felt like a man after what I had just been through.

Mixed feelings were now setting in. There was a real sense of satisfaction – but I was still gutted. Those words 'if only' were worming their way inside me. I wasn't telling people around me yet but I was 90 per cent sure I was going to quit now. The problem was the other 10 per cent of me.

The statistics showed that I had given one of the greatest fighters in the history of the middleweight division a real scare. He had thrown 691 punches to my 408 but I had landed a better percentage, 38 per cent to 30. I had landed more jabs as well, 79 to his 68. To be fair, he had landed more power punches than I had, however: 138 to my 76.

It told me that I could compete at the highest level and it would be a shame to waste that experience. I had also not achieved my mission of winning a world title for Gary. Did I want to – could I – go through all of this again, though?

As I necked my beer and watched people playing at the card tables, listening to the consolation and compliments of friends and family, I asked myself the big question. Do I stick or twist?

III

BACK WITH THE WORLD

Everything dies baby that's a fact,
But maybe everything that dies, some day comes back.
Put your make-up on, fix your hair up pretty,
And meet me tonight in Atlantic City.

Atlantic City
Bruce Springsteen

21

THE PRICE OF PAIN

The bloke in the passport control booth at Heathrow Airport asked me to take my sunglasses off.

"Bloody hell," he said taking one look at the black eyes that were still healing these couple of days after the Martinez fight. "What happened to you?"

"You should have seen the other geezer," I replied and explained where I'd been and what I'd been doing. He sympathised, we both laughed and he waved me on my way even if I didn't quite look like my photo.

It was less of a joke when I went to Gemma's Mum's to pick up Scarlett. Now almost 10 months old, she looked at me suspiciously, almost as if she was saying: "Well, you sound like my Dad but you don't look like him." It upset me and I never wanted her to see me like this again.

I had gone round to Southgate to collect her as the first thing I did after getting home, ahead of the rest of the family, as I had been booked on an earlier overnight flight. When they all got back, it felt great. I was among those who loved me, having achieved more than I ever thought I would in boxing, and I was receiving generous comments from within boxing both in England and in the States. The American promoter Lou Di Bella, for example, told me I had done myself proud and now had a box office presence in America.

The money came through within a week, with Eddie as good

as his word in promising that I would be paid promptly, unlike with some other promoters. After the advance against my purse was taken out, along with the tax deduction at source, I was left with about £150,000, from which Tony was paid his well-earned share. Then there were debts to settle, like for my hip operation, and I also wanted to pay off some domestic back tax.

After a nice holiday for me, Gemma and Scarlett in Dubai at the luxurious One&Only Royal Mirage Hotel that Eddie had booked for us, I came back and worked out how to spend the money I was left with. One thing was for sure: I wasn't going to waste it.

And so we bought that semi-detached bungalow in East Barnet with a garden, half a mile away from the maisonette we had pretty much grown out of. Although we got £275,000 for the maisonette, I still needed a sizeable mortgage because the place needed a lot of doing up, and though my family, mainly Dad, Grandad, Uncle Dean and Gem's Dad Charlie, were going to help out with all the work, the cost of materials was still plenty.

Getting a mortgage was not easy, though, given that it was difficult to prove my income, what with its irregular nature due to all the injuries I'd had. There were also doubts over what I might do next. It took a couple of applications, in fact.

I may have fought for a world title but I was far from rich and could not yet own my own home outright. At least I had something to show from boxing, as I was determined to do, although it would take a while to move in as the place was being done up. We were grateful to Gem's parents for putting us up for the time being. Charlie and Janet were always good to us.

If you think about the £150,000 I had cleared for the Martinez fight, it came six months after the £25,000 net from the Spada fight and together these paydays represented my total earnings for 18 months. And I didn't know when I would be earning again. That said, I always maintained I would have fought Martinez for much, much less. I just wanted that shot.

I was still going to the gym on and off for a couple of months but still hadn't worked out what to do with my future when the fifth anniversary of Gary's death arrived. We always marked the day by getting together as a family and down the years we would go for a meal and a day out together, to places like the South Bank in London, St Albans Cathedral, or to Brighton.

Also, on his birthday in the February each year, we would write messages to Gary on helium balloons, to express our love to and for him, then we'd let them loose into the night sky. Mum would also get a cake for him. The idea was just to acknowledge the days of his death and birthday and swap stories of our loved one. It was never going to be easy but we grew a bit more talkative each year.

Scarlett's first birthday soon followed, and after Christmas, and when the New Year of 2012 arrived, it was time to make my next move – if there was to be one.

The previous year had been a good year. I'd had two fights and with neither of them did I really have that depression in mid-training camp where I went into the deep black holes of old. That dream I had – God-given, Tony and I reckoned – almost urging me to give it another go and do it for Gary, had driven me on.

No matter how well training camps go, though, and even having Tony alongside me the whole time, to which I could add Lee, Mark and Luke in Canada, it is a tough, lonely sport, and those three months of sacrifice and single-mindedness are brutal and gruelling.

At first, it's like a footballer starting off pre-season, doing the running to get a fitness base. I was up at 5.30 am and running five to seven miles, mixing it up for variety by either doing it on the roads around my home or near Tony's gym in Essex. On two mornings a week, I would do sprint or track work then go up for a sleep on the bed Tony had installed in the office above his gym before the afternoon session.

Then there would be the shadow boxing, the bag and pad work and the skipping - half an hour of each - with a spell on an exercise bike to warm down. That was as well as the sparring that was introduced after a month or so, starting with one-minute rounds and building up to five minutes per round. Lots of them.

Once a week, I would have a strength and condition session with a trainer, at that time Chris Kemp, over in Essex. Tony would give me Wednesday mornings and Saturdays off and on Sundays I would do my own run near my home to keep ticking over, ready to start again on the Monday.

It wasn't so much all the training, though, as at least I could enjoy the camaraderie of the gym with Tony's growing stable of boxers, good men like Lee Purdy, Ryan Taylor and Martin Ward. It was more the privations of going without food that got to me most. Even at this stage of my career, having fought for a world title, my diet was not as good as it should have been, I have to admit.

People just don't see or appreciate what boxers have to go through to make their fighting weight and for a big middleweight like me, it was especially tough.

Very soon after a fight, I would grow to 13 stones and so need to lose 22 lbs over the course of a 12-week training camp to make the middleweight limit. The idea was to lose at most 3 lbs a week rather than crash diet. Some weeks I might not lose any weight and would get worried.

You lived your life on and off the scales with Tony frequently checking you, although I could tell my weight more or less, knowing my own body. Sometimes I would put my hands round my waist at weekends and know what I was going to weigh on Monday morning.

Two weeks before a fight, I would expect to be under 12 stones, probably 11st 11lbs, and if I was still three or four pounds over on the Monday before a weekend fight, I wouldn't be too worried, knowing I could lose that, even if it was still tough.

There were times, however, particularly when I was struggling with my hips, when I might be 7lbs over with a week to go and I would get very worried, frightened even, as I would be drained from the lack of food. I always made it, somehow, but never without agonies, it always seemed.

Tony trusted me to eat properly because if I hadn't stuck to my plan, the regular visits to the scales would tell him and it would be me who had to suffer. The plan was to eat little and often, starting with porridge in the morning then eating such foods as chicken, steak and pasta, but all in small quantities. Boxers also get paranoid about their fluid intake. I was always worried about drinking too much water and putting on weight but of course you sweat it off.

Sometimes I would give in to the hunger pangs and raid the cupboard, then had to lose four pounds over the next day or two. The main problem was always Friday night round my Mum and Dad's house - fish and chips night. I suppose I shouldn't have gone sometimes but the twin attractions of family and food usually proved irresistible.

I was mostly good about the fish and, rather than batter, went for the healthier option of having it cooked in matzo meal, which is a form of breadcrumbs and used a lot in Jewish cooking. There were plenty of chip shops in North London where it was sold. No, the problem was always the two tons of chips floating around, and the chances of me not having any were very slim.

What got me most, though, was that if I had had a good week and signed off from the gym ahead of my weight schedule and so a bit light on a Friday, I would eat a whole fish and chips portion. Then I would be several pounds over on a Monday morning and panic, and before I knew it my depression would kick in again.

It could be even worse the closer you got to a fight, with the rations being mean and meagre. You were still allowed steak and chicken but tiny portions, and just with salad. You could get light headed. I hated the whole bloody weight thing and I don't know a boxer who didn't.

Then there were the injuries. The doctor had always said that the right hip would probably need an operation some time in the future, but the future was sooner that I thought. It had started giving me gyp in those last days before the Martinez fight and I wasn't sure now how long it would hold out.

I talked it all over in what might be described as crunch talks with Tony and Eddie at one of the terrific barbecues Matchroom do for staff and fighters over at Mascalls. I said I was thinking of packing it in. Barry Hearn was also there. Tony would never put any pressure on me but like Eddie and Barry, who were more forceful, he asked me what I was going to do instead. Eddie wondered if I fancied working on a building site. Or driving a black cab.

I was always confident I would make a living in whatever I chose to do, I said. I had shown a dedication and determination through adversity and reckoned I could use those same qualities to succeed in another field. I had ideas - maybe a bit of TV work, maybe some personal training based on boxing fitness work.

Eddie sounded sceptical and I was a bit annoyed, to be honest. I thought they were underestimating me. Then I thought through what he was saying. He felt I had come so far that it would be a shame to waste of all that work in building my reputation. I had a lot more to give, he said.

To be fair to Eddie, I trusted him when he said his opinion was not based on what he might earn out of me but on my own future financial wellbeing. He did have a point. In fact, he and Tony both did when they said it would be good to be mortgage free and own my house outright, and that boxing could do that for me.

On top of all that, Lou Di Bella had told me that my stock had gone through the roof in America and Martinez himself had been very complimentary to me. We communicated on Twitter now with the mutual respect of warriors who had shared a ring.

I was one of the last to get the best of Sergio, I reckon. After me running him so close, more opponents were now coming out wanting to take him on. He would go on to beat Matt Macklin, also in the 11th, then Julio Cesar Chavez Jnr and Martin Murray on points before losing to Miguel Cotto in the summer of 2014 at Madison Square Garden after being out of the ring for more than a year. He would announce his retirement finally in the summer of 2015.

It niggled at me: I could have beaten him that night. I was proud of myself and my performance, and had basked in it these past few months, but I had still lost. When I really could have taken him. He just had more nous at the crucial times and that was the decisive difference. I had fought the best of the best, a future hall-of-famer, and had not been outclassed.

It would, contemplating all the options, be a shame to cut and run now, I could see. I was more marketable now and there were some big fights out there for me, be it domestic level with the middleweight scene vibrant, at European and World levels.

And, to be honest, the potential money I could now command was appealing. The Martinez purse was great, but it was not life-changing. The costs of doing up the bungalow the way we wanted it were increasing, as well.

I went back to the gym to tell Tony I was going to give it another go. He was pleased I had come to my senses but more that I was not going to waste my potential. I then rang Eddie to ask him to get me another fight.

He was straight on the case and weaved a bit more of his magic. Soon he was lining me up to face the Russian Dmitry Pirog for the WBO middleweight crown on the HBO network in America again. It may not have been such a prestigious title, being for one of the lesser governing bodies, nor such a glamorous opponent as Sergio Martinez, but it was a world title fight once more and it rekindled my enthusiasm. I was going to be looking at a good sum too, if not quite the Martinez numbers.

Back in the gym, I knuckled down. I had motivation anew, in getting my house done up and paid for, in taking care of Gem and Scarlett, and in fulfilling that promise of winning a world title for Gary's memory.

This was Darren Barker we were talking about, though. It was never going to be that simple. My sponsor and special mate Luke Chandler will tell you all about that and what we went through…

22

LUKE

Luke Chandler was born on the Isle of Sheppey in Kent in 1978, the youngest of three children, his two sisters six and two years older than him respectively. His parents having split up before he was 10 years old, Luke was raised in pubs by his licensee father. He admits getting into plenty of fights as a teenager but because he was big for his age, eventually other kids refused to fight him.

After leaving school he became a scaffolder, then set up his own company in 2005, Elite Scaffolding, driven by a desire to be his own man and a successful businessman. Based in Kent, he is a family man with two young sons.

As a manual worker, he had been consuming up to 6,000 calories a day but was burning them off in shifting up to 15 tons of scaffolding material. A few years into running his growing company, he was still consuming large numbers of calories, his weight rising to 17 stones, and he decided he needed to get fit. He spoke to his friend Mark Seltzer, who was then married to Luke's wife's best friend. Mark, Tony Sims's corner man, told Luke that Tony did personal boxing training for amateurs as well as working with professionals.

Luke was uncertain at first. He had always loved boxing, recalling being fascinated by the brutal Nigel Benn-Gerald McClellan fight that left McClellan blind and brain-damaged, but his experiences at a local boxing club when a teenager left him sceptical about boxers.

That feeling would soon depart, once he met Tony Sims and Darren Barker. Luke would also have an issue with one of his sisters that gave him some insight into the kind of sadness around siblings that both Tony and Darren had undergone…

"I had been to a boxing club on Sheppey but there were some real bullies there. Not nice people. I've since found out that happens a lot until the discipline and the code that boxers need weeds the bullies out when they find they are not up to it. To this day, I hate bullying, physical or verbal.

At Tony's gym, I found a different group and atmosphere altogether, men who changed my perception of fighters. Tony made sure he had good characters as well as good boxers. In fact, from the day I walked in up to now, I don't think I have met a boxer who was a bad man. They have a set of morals that make them the men they are. You see who they are, what they go through and you fall in love with them.

I took to Tony straight away and he became a calming influence on me, as he still is today. The few hours I spent with him took me away from the madness of reality. I also got to know and understand Bryn Robertson who was training there and I enjoyed his company.

Within three sessions Tony told me he was looking for a sponsor and I jumped on the opportunity. I had met some of the boxers, like Lee Purdy and Danny Cadman, and I was beginning to understand the finances of boxing at that level, what they were putting themselves through. They were at British level and not getting much money. There isn't much until you get to European or World level. I started helping Tony out with the rent and giving the fighters petrol cards, that sort of thing.

I got more into it and starting going away with the boys for a few days on their training camps. I hadn't known Darren all that long – I started with Tony just after Darren had won the British title by beating Danny Butler - when I went on a training camp in Tenerife with him and Tony and some of the others. He had not long beaten Affif Belghecham to win the European title and was lining up a fight with Matthew Macklin.

One day I watched him break down during his running and

it was painful to see. He was normally a really good runner. That night he sat down with me by the pool and wanted to talk. Our relationship was still young and tender and usually it would take years to know someone well enough to talk the way we did but we just clicked instantly.

He said he couldn't go through this any more. He was in bits, worried about his future and what else he could do with his life because boxing was over for him. "It's my hips. They're shot," he said and he kept repeating it. I asked him if he'd had them looked at and he said there was no point. They were just shot. He couldn't do the running he needed to be fit for fights. I knew how important this was. Despite modern methods and technology, a fighter still has to have the miles in his legs.

The thought of Darren quitting did not sit well with me. People said Gary was the one with the talent and Darren was the one who had to work hard but he had a real talent too.

I got called back to the UK on business and sat on the plane brooding about it. I was almost depressed. When I got back, I thought I had to do something because nobody else was. At that time, I don't think there was enough embracing of science and medical help, even if Tony could adapt the training.

I rang my private doctor in London and he recommended a hip specialist. Before Darren had even got back from Tenerife, I had booked him in for a consultation and an X-ray. I was happy to pay the £1,800 just to get him sorted.

I was elated when Dr Johan Witt said he could fix this and quickly. Darren was down because he had to go under the knife. While we had so much in common – including us both being hypochondriacs - we had different approaches to things being wrong with us. I wanted to know what the problem was and get it fixed. Darren would sit and worry more about it.

Getting his hip fixed was never going to be the end of the problems with Darren, mind. As well as a lot of other physical stuff, he always had the mental side of things to go through as well.

I suppose there was also a synergy between us because of what had happened with my younger sister. My older sister is an angel. She provides respite care for families with problem children by taking the kids for a weekend so that the parents can get a break. My other sister has had a lot of problems, though. She was a self-made woman, buying and selling houses, but she had poor taste in men and had a breakdown.

I paid a lot of money around Christmas 2009 to put her through a clinic but she left after three weeks without completing the programme. That scarred our relationship. Then six months later, we lost our father and she caused so many problems over the estate that we haven't spoken since.

In a way, I have lost a sibling as well. I've heard about the bond Darren had with Gary, and seen the bond he has with Lee, and I wished I'd had a brother. When I said that to him once, he said: "You have now," and that meant a lot to me.

I've watched Darren go through all sorts of highs and lows down the years, seen his dark days and been with him through the good times, holidays in Spain, Vegas. I've had my down days too. Watching him get hit. It's hard when it's someone you love.

And to be honest, I don't think I've ever got any business out of my sponsorship. The TV exposure doesn't do it. In my world, my business comes through reputation and word of mouth. I've taken the odd client into the dressing rooms down the years but that's about the only benefit I've had. You can't claim a lot back on tax. Your profit's your profit.

All that said, I would have paid it 10 times over for the memories and the moments and the laughs we've had. There are so many things I've done in life that I have forgotten about or where my memory is cloudy but I have unforgettable recollections of times I've had with Darren. A song will come on the radio and we will look at each other and have a memory of some place, on holiday or in a training camp somewhere, where we heard it before.

There was the training camp in Canada before the Martinez fight… being in Darren's dressing room... sitting in the front row ringside with Eddie. I never liked to drink before his fights. I liked to take it all in, have all my senses clear.

Then when you think of all he went through – the injuries and these black holes he sank into. Sometimes it felt like he was going to war against heavy weapons with just a hand gun. At one point before the Martinez fight, he couldn't run, and could barely snap out a jab. And he was about to take on one of the most feared fighters on the planet. Tony asked me to have a word with him and we spoke for an hour, just trying to shift his mood. I don't know what it was, but I grasped Darren and his moods.

Most people have their down sides. But I can honestly say that with him, he's not got a bad point. I can say nothing negative about him. The only down side he's shown me is the things that trouble him when he is low.

Two things affect performance: the way you live your life between camps and the way you train. Darren didn't live the life for many years. He was eating badly and going through despair.

It means that reaching the top, even for one fight, for one night, takes some doing. But he kept doing it, no matter the setbacks.”

23

NEW TROUBLES, NEW ATTITUDE

We were running in Hainault Forest near Tony's gym, me and some of the other guys, when it happened. My right hip had gone now. I knew it straight away, because it felt so similar to when the left one had given me so much pain. That feeling of the bone grinding in the socket and the excruciating pain. I could only walk slowly back to the gym. When I got there, as soon as I started telling Tony what had happened, I broke down in tears.

It would be the end of the Pirog fight and the payday that went with it. I was distraught. I had now run out of money, in buying and doing up the bungalow, and work had stopped on it. Gem, Scarlett and I were grateful to Gem's Mum and Dad for continuing to put us up at their house in Southgate but it was not ideal, either for them or for us.

Thankfully, Tony kept a calm head when I needed one and helped to lift my spirits. He reminded me that I had had the left hip done and come back so I knew I could do it again. The episode just seemed to highlight my problem, though: I was either physically well but not mentally, or mentally OK but not physically. That was always the struggle for me.

As a sportsman, you are always battling against an opponent – quite literally in boxing - but you are also always constantly battling with yourself. That is the struggle behind the scenes that few people see. Fight night was fine. That was the time to shine. It was everything leading up to it…

I went to see the same surgeon, Dr Johan Witt, and pretty much knew he was going to tell me I needed another operation. The left hip was holding up, but as a result, the deficiencies in the right one were being exposed more. I was less anxious this time, having resigned myself to needing more surgery one day, and knowing the operation involved. In fact, I found it all almost laughable by this point. I had been hoping that the process could be delayed until after I had finished boxing but it wasn't going to happen.

This time, Bryn Robertson, who had seen me in pain in the gym and sympathised with my plight, helped me by paying half of the £8,000 cost.

Again the operation went well but it is a horrible feeling coming out of the surgery. You know then that you are going to be on crutches for a month and you can't do anything much. Inactivity and patience have never been my strong suits. The only exercise I could do was another round of the follow-up hydrotherapy at the private hospital just off Harley Street, just basic movements up and down the pool.

After the month of rehab in the pool, I was able to walk without the crutches but there was still little fitness work I could do as you can't go jumping up and down on a hip joint that's still healing. I enjoyed some home time with Scarlett and made sure I was still out and about, not sitting at home vegetating in front of the TV. But I still grew frustrated, and depressed at times, as I brooded once more on whether this was going to be the end or whether I could go through all that was required to get back in the ring even if I did get fit again. By now, my weight was pushing 14 stones, the heaviest I had ever been, and it was getting me down.

That mood probably contributed again to my getting into a few scrapes. Again, none of the episodes was my fault but the fact that I was involved, if not as an instigator, showed that I was getting myself in the wrong place at the wrong time. I was just trying to have some fun with my mates, once I was at least mobile.

On the first occasion, I was out in the West End of London with some mates – Daisy's boyfriend Sean, Ben Levy and his brother Jack – and we were walking up the Charing Cross Road next to Piccadilly tube station minding our own business when Jack accidentally bumped into a guy. Jack, a lovely, peaceful guy, apologised but the bloke wasn't having any of it and started ranting, telling Jack he would stab him.

Ben was quickly in to defend his brother and nutted the guy. One of the bloke's mates then came at me as a free-for-all broke out. I just hit him with a left hook and he landed, star shape, on the steps of Piccadilly station.

After that, we made off smartly but only got a few hundred yards, as far as Leicester Square, when we had to stop for Sean, who looked to have come off worst with a dislocated shoulder. It was unlucky. He reckoned it was the first time he had ever hit anybody. He was a lover not a fighter.

It was then that the police caught up with us. Maybe they saw it all on CCTV and had officers in the area because they got to us quickly. I for one was easily spotted as I was wearing a long grey jacket. Sean turned out to be the lucky one. He got to spend the night in hospital. I spent it in a cell again, at Charing Cross police station.

I had that same claustrophobic feeling as that night in Watford around the first anniversary of Gary's death, in that confined space with just a hard bed, a basin and a toilet for company. But I was more used to it this time and knew it would be useless to try and talk my way out of it. Still, it was another restless night before they let me off with a caution in the morning.

There was another time when we ended up in a pizza place up West again and someone pushed into the queue ahead of us. It all kicked off but was nowhere near as bad as the previous time. The police were called but thankfully we were all just given spot fines of £70 each this time, even if I hated forking out.

What is it with some people? A few drinks and they think they are a small army. Maybe it is because me and my friends dress well and they think they can take us but they pick on the wrong guys. I would never go looking for trouble, hate street fighting and try to get out of it – it's a bit like taking your work home with you, after all – but if someone starts it by throwing their weight around, I for one am not going to put up with it.

That said, there was a time when I probably did over-react. I was queuing with mates outside a nightclub when two blokes pushed in front of the people in front of us. When those two questioned it, the others wondered what they were going to do about it. I found myself getting involved and chinned them. It soon got broken up by bouncers and the two who had pushed in got pulled away. Not before he had launched a bottle at me, hitting me on the back and leaving a big bruise.

It was all a bit mental and I was not proud of myself. On the first two occasions I was simply defending mates. With this one, I didn't know what came over me. I just wouldn't back down. I guess I could be stubborn like that sometimes.

The time came to get back to some proper fighting but although my hips were now fixed, supposedly, it would still not be simple. A fight was arranged, with Eddie and Tony securing Simone Rotolo of Italy for the IBF International title, a stepping stone to another world title fight. The date was fixed for September, just after the London Olympic Games, at Alexandra Palace and the posters went out with me top of the bill.

Off we went to a training camp in Spain, me, Tony, fitness coach Chris Kemp and stablemates Lee Purdy, Ryan Taylor and Martin Ward. They went running on the roads while I ran on a treadmill, the impact being less harsh. I also did some swimming. I enjoyed the camaraderie again but was still a creature of habit and missed my routine at home.

It was when we got back in the gym at home that it all went wrong again. I was sparring one day with Diego Burton, a hard-as-nails Peckham fighter – so hard that even during Ramadan when, being a Muslim, he was not allowed to eat or drink during the day, he still sparred, and just for a £50 fee. Anyway, as I threw a body shot, I took an elbow in my bicep followed by a punch there. It was all accidental on Diego's part but I had to stop the spar.

Tony sent me up to Harley Street to see Dr Mike Loosemore, the private GP he used for his boxers, and it turned out that the bicep was ruptured. I wanted to try and let it heal for a week or two and go ahead with the fight against Rotolo but the medical advice was that it would be madness.

I was devastated. Yet again. I was doing well with the weight and the venue of Ally Pally, and the occasion, would be the perfect setting for a comeback after a year out of the ring. I was furious and took it out on someone I shouldn't have.

I went up to the West End with my mate Waheed and got drunk. We started arguing over something, and it went on all the while we walked the couple of miles from Tottenham Court Road to Camden Town. It wasn't like me. Waheed was a great guy. It was a sign of how pissed and pissed off I was.

That, I told everyone after getting the diagnosis of a ruptured bicep, was me finished. Once more. I was sick of all the injuries and the setbacks. I had been offered some personal training work at the gym at Chelsea Football Club and that would keep me ticking over for now.

Then one day that Autumn, I stood with Gem's Dad Charlie and my Grandad in the shell of the bungalow and they took me through every area of the house and outlined to me the thousands of pounds it would take to get it in a decent shape. It was going to take me years as a personal trainer to pay for all that. In fact, no ordinary job was going to earn me that amount of money.

I spent another night on the sofa with Scarlett crying – her, not me, though I knew how she felt - and by the morning, I had come to a conclusion. I needed the money. I was going to go back and this time, as well as being for Gary, I was going to do it now as much for the money.

I drove over to the gym to see Tony. I told him that I was going to give this one more chance and go at it with all guns blazing. Or, to be more accurate, I was going to give my body one more chance. The bicep duly healed and I went back into training.

Tony and Eddie again did their best for me and arranged a comeback fight against the Welshman Kerry Hope in the December of 2012, just a couple of days ahead of the sixth anniversary of Gary's death. This time I couldn't go straight back in at the top to contest a title. After 15 months out of the ring – and just two fights in two and a half years – I needed a warm-up fight. And while it may have been in a lower key after the high notes of the Sergio Martinez fight, it would still bring its own questions and pressures.

How rusty would I be? How much toll would the injuries have taken? All this on top of the regular fears that boxers have about getting hurt and whether a beating might mean the end of a career. Training camps are also always the same no matter who you are fighting. The issue in my case was whether I would get through one. I would just have to take it one day at a time.

Hope, another southpaw, was a decent opponent, too. He had won the European Middleweight crown in the March by outpointing Grezegorz Proksa of Poland but then lost it on a cut in a rematch four months later. Hope was only 31 as well, and was looking to get himself back up the world rankings and in line for a title fight, so he was a dangerous opponent.

Training went as well as could be hoped, given my restrictions. I could really do my running only on the treadmill and I was still getting pain in my elbows, particularly the left one, when I snapped out the jab. Dr Loosemore gave me a cortisone injection and it helped plenty. It would wear off, though, in the months to come and I would need another. And another. In all, I had no fewer than seven, four in the left elbow, over a three-year period. I don't think you're supposed to have more than three in a lifetime.

I guess the paying public had their doubts about whether I would be fit enough to fight, given that I had had to pull out of bills before, so ticket sales were not as good as they might have been. This was also despite my mate Dave Johnstone of the CFCUK fanzine rounding up as many Chelsea fans as possible. In fact, Olympia being such a big arena, parts of it would be curtained off so that it didn't look empty.

It was going to be an anxious night in more ways than one as I contemplated again being the forgotten man of the middleweight division with Andy Lee, Matt Macklin and Martin Murray now getting the big fights. It seemed I was no longer box office and that thought irked me.

I had always had a lot of trust in Tony and Eddie and I never asked what I might be getting for this fight, the arrangement being that it would be agreed when we saw how the ticket sales had gone. Even though I knew this was not a big revenue-generating bill, I was a bit taken aback in the dressing room beforehand when Tony told me, as he was going through the wrapping of my hands in bandages, that I would be getting £20,000 for the fight. Twenty grand? It didn't touch the surface of what I needed, what with my debts and everything that still needed doing to the bungalow.

As a fighter, you always think you deserve more. If anyone in sport earns their money, it is boxers. You are putting your health, even your life, on the line. Tony thought he had done well for me and got me a reasonable deal considering everything, and I am sure that was all Eddie could afford to pay me, but I have to admit I was pissed off.

Boxers try to avoid fighting angry because it can leave you open to attack, quite literally, if you are not using your head as well as your heart. You want to be in control of the aggression. I fought angry that night, though. Coupled with my new mentality about coming out with guns blazing, I was formidable.

At first my timing was off and it took me a couple of rounds to get back into the groove as I used just my jab to try and build up a lead. Then in the third, I caught him with a sharp combination and it softened him up for the fourth, when I got him with a big overhand right.

He went down near the ropes and I knew I had him. He beat the count but was so groggy that his corner threw in the towel straight away. I was glad it was over. No messing about with getting a proper test and some rounds under my belt. I was a man on a mission. I wanted to earn that £20,000 as quickly as I could.

It was the most spiteful I had ever been in the ring and I actually found myself wanting to hurt my opponent. Perhaps Tony had mentioned the money only in the dressing room thinking that maybe I needed some motivation, so that I would come out firing on all cylinders, but I was in the mood anyway.

I had lost so much time and, having turned 30 earlier that year, I knew I only had a few more years and fights, given how my body was being patched up. Personally, I was delighted by the Hope performance and reckoned that it signalled a new instinct and no-nonsense approach in me.

After every fight in recent years, I had thought of calling it a day because the mental side of boxing, in going through the training and with pain, so often got me down. Now that I knew that every fight could be my last, for physical reasons, I had resolved to give it everything I could and had a much more aggressive attitude.

Having come through a training camp without any more damage and won a fight convincingly, I was ready now to get on with things and asked Eddie to get me another fight as quickly as he could.

It would come early the next year, in the March of 2013, which meant two fights in four months and me being as active as I had been for years. A title would be on the line this time as well. The IBF International Middleweight belt wasn't a big deal, I have to admit, but it would improve my ranking if I won, would project me high in the rankings with the IBF and thus put me in contention for another world title fight.

Besides, it was another belt, a nice looking one, and more memorabilia for Dad's growing boxing exhibition at the family home. As a kid, I always loved getting a trophy after every bout. As a pro, I still loved all the belts.

I had asked Eddie if he could get me another shot at Simone Rotolo as I felt I had unfinished business dating back to the European title fight back in September. Eddie delivered again and made the match for Wembley Arena.

It was another milestone for me, being my first fight at Wembley, one of those venues every kid dreams of performing at. Boxers aren't too much different to footballers in that. It would also be in the same hall as where my Dad won his ABA title back in 1980. The event was billed as 'London's Finest' and would also feature my stable mate Lee Purdy and the confident, up-and-coming George Groves, who just had signed a short-term promotional deal with Eddie.

As well as bringing together Barker and Rotolo, there was a match of another sort in the run-up to the night. Eddie had asked me to do some press work at Wembley Stadium to promote the event and I took the chance to do something special. I asked Gemma to come along with me on the day and she agreed. Then I went and had a word with the people there who operated the scoreboard.

As we were out on the pitch, up it came on to the screen – "Will you marry me, Gemma?" It was signed off with an X for a kiss. Luckily there were no football fans in the place or they might have chanted: "You don't know what you're doing." Luckily, too, she said yes. It was the day before Valentine's, so I had managed to get myself in her good books.

When it came to the Rotolo match a few weeks later, there was no love lost and I would end up not respecting him as an opponent. This time, though, I was happy enough with the money, having been told well in advance what I would be getting, roughly double the Hope money. I was also delighted to be top of the bill.

I had a scare on the morning of the weigh-in when I checked my weight ahead of the official ceremony and I was a few ounces over. I was annoyed because I had made it through training, working on with the usual injury niggles, and then this. There was always something. I was concerned because there was not a sliver of fat on me. I was drawn to nothing.

Also, I always worked hard on coming in bang on the weight and I didn't want to take the risk of that excruciating feeling of being embarrassed in front of everyone when you haven't made the weight. Scales can also differ in various locations and I didn't want to take that risk of being too close to the limit.

And so I turned up the heating in my room in the Hilton Hotel across the road and got a sweat on by doing some skipping. Fortunately, it worked. I was a comfortable 14 ounces under the limit, seven less than my opponent.

On the night, with the same attitude I had shown against Kerry Hope, I tore into Rotolo from the first bell and knocked him over with a combination of punches towards the end of the first round.

After that, I thought I could get him quickly with a knockout or a stoppage but it became a messy contest, mainly because he hadn't come to fight but to cling on. In the fourth round, I caught him with another flurry and he backed off, shaking a hand in pain, though I didn't think he was badly hurt. He just had no stomach for it, in my opinion. In the break before the fifth, his corner pulled him out.

It was fine with me. I may not have got the chance to impress and give my fans and Sky Sports some extended entertainment – and more beyond the barmy Barker army from Barnet were coming back now, more convinced that my fights would be going ahead – but a win was a win and would reposition me back in the elite middleweight shake-up.

Then something strange happened to me as I started doing my TV interview. Although Rotolo had hardly laid a glove on me, I began to see stars in front of my eyes. I had no peripheral vision and could see only what was in front of me. I got a lift home from the family but on the short trip home from Wembley to East Barnet, I also felt sick.

I was worried but it felt a bit better the next morning and thankfully the eye trouble passed over the next few days. It must have been down either to losing some weight the day before or being caught a glancing blow in a vulnerable area of the head.

I didn't want to go and see a doctor in case they stopped me boxing for the foreseeable future. And now there were some big fights on the horizon, with me being back in the game, ranked in the top 10 with all the major governing bodies and even in the top five of the IBF.

Before I fought again, I would try my hand at something new – being a trainer. Eddie had lined up an IBF World Welterweight title fight for Lee Purdy in the May against Devon Alexander in Atlantic City. Lee, as game as anything, took the fight at four weeks' notice because Kell Brook had to pull out with a hand injury.

It turned out that Tony Sims was unable to travel with Lee for some personal reasons and he asked me if I would work Lee's corner on the night. He didn't know, he said, anyone as close to Lee that both he and Lee trusted. I had the knowledge, both of a world title fight and the venue, which was to be Boardwalk Hall. Tony would be in constant touch with me and I would have his brother Peter, a trainer himself, and Mark Selzer with me in the build-up. Eddie would also be coming out for the fight.

I was reluctant, given my inexperience, but agreed, as a favour to two men I loved and respected and spent every day of my working life with. And I would come to see from the other side of the ropes just how tough a job training is – and how emotionally involved you become with your fighter.

During a short training camp in Toronto, and then after going on to New York, for some media work, and in Atlantic City, it became obvious how much Lee was struggling to make the weight. He was on a special diet plan and it was difficult trailing round places trying to get the right ingredients for him.

When we finally got to Atlantic City, it became clear that was not going to come in under the 147 lbs limit despite all his best efforts. He starved himself and tried to sweat everything out but there was just not a spare ounce on him. In the end, he was as dry as a bone and exhausted.

I was worried about him the night before the weigh-in as he shut himself in his room and just lay on the bed. I was texting him at regular intervals, just to check on him. I felt for him and would have gone the rounds with Devon Alexander myself if I could have rather than see Lee like this.

As we went down in the lift for the weigh-in at Caesar's Palace, where we were staying, I told Lee to put back his shoulders and not to show on his face the struggles he had gone through. I know myself that your opponent gets a real lift if he sees you have struggled to make the weight. But it was no good. The poor bloke could barely stand and needed help.

He came in at a pound over and was given two hours to shed the weight. Enough was enough. There was none to be shed, certainly not at that short notice, and any more physical exercise would have been cruel. Barry Hearn was also out there and negotiated with Alexander's promoters, Golden Boy.

In the end a deal was done. The fight would go ahead but it

would be non-title and Lee would forfeit 10 per cent of his purse. I told him not to worry, to puff out his chest and put on a good show in the ring anyway.

Lee could then eat a hearty meal and he suddenly became a different man overnight. Come the fight itself, though, the regime he had endured, and the fact that his training camp had been short, quickly took its toll.

Now Lee – who retired after one more fight, when he lost in challenging for the European title - was one of the most honest boxers there could be, a throwback all-action type. He could take a punch and he could deliver one all right. Watching him against Alexander that night as the early rounds unfolded, though, I grew anxious. He was taking too many punches and not looking as if he was going to land a telling one himself.

After six rounds, I thought he was being well beaten and I didn't want my friend to take too much punishment. Tony was watching at home on TV and was on the phone all the time to Ryan Taylor, who had come out there with us and was in a seat near our corner, and Ryan was relaying Tony's thoughts and instructions to me. In the end, though, I was the man responsible.

By the end of the seventh, I had seen enough and pulled Lee out. He was initially unhappy with my decision but came to accept that I was acting in his best interests. It was a tough dilemma – wanting to give your fighter every chance but not wanting to see him hurt.

I also got some stick from British boxing fans for my decision. They reckoned Alexander was not hurting Lee. I was close up and could see the punishment, though. And I knew what had gone on in the days leading up to the fight in a way that they had not. This training stuff was tough and at that time I thought it was not for me.

That viewpoint was reinforced shortly after we got back when we were all summoned to the British Boxing Board of Control's office at London Bridge for a disciplinary hearing. When out in America, Eddie had tweeted that Lee was having a hard time with his weight and one fan replied asking if we had tried a sauna. Eddie's response was that we'd tried everything.

The Board were made aware of it and interpreted it as Lee using a sauna, a practice they frown on because it can dehydrate and weaken a fighter in the lead-in to a fight. I could understand that but all fighters are different and some can tolerate it. It is also difficult to monitor and I know some fighters who have had them 24 hours before and been fine. I also liked a sauna just because it made me feel good but I understood and respected the concern about the issues too close to a fight

Anyway, the board wanted to fine Lee, who was represented by Tony at the hearing, over £20,000, me £5,000 and Eddie £2,000. In the end, Eddie paid up for the jokey tweet he sent but Tony argued that Lee had already been punished in America by losing part of his purse and that I had done nothing wrong. They accepted his reasoning and the case was dismissed.

I wanted to get back to my bit of the boxing business that I knew and did best. When we were out in Canada and America, I had accompanied Lee in training to keep up my own fitness as I knew that Eddie was getting busy on my behalf.

There were new chances of good pay days with maybe Macklin or Murray domestically but I still hadn't found what I was really looking for - another world championship shot that would give me the chance to deliver on my promise to Gary and to get the bungalow sorted too. It may have been a bit of a nightmare trip with Lee to the States but I was all for going back there if Eddie could get me another tilt at that crown.

24

EDDIE

Eddie Hearn fell in love with boxing at a time when his father Barry was enjoying a period of promoting the sport in the late 1980s and 1990s amid all his work at the time with his Matchroom company in making snooker one of the most talked-about sports in Britain. At the age of eight, in 1987, Eddie attended the first fight his Dad arranged, indeed - Frank Bruno v Joe Bugner at White Hart Lane.

After that, Eddie grew up around Nigel Benn, Chris Eubank and Naseem Hamed and boxed himself for a couple of his teenage years, contesting three amateur bouts, at Billericay Boys Club in Essex, near the public school he attended.

As he himself says, though: "The fact is, when you go to a public school and your Dad's a millionaire, you're never going to be a fighter. It's not in you."

The public school concerned was Brentwood, near the family home – Mascalls, which is now the Matchroom headquarters. The footballer Frank Lampard was in the year above Eddie at Brentwood.

"I was a horrible brat at school," he says. "A Jack the lad, leader of the school, which wasn't hard because 99.9 per cent of them were born with a silver spoon in their mouth. I had a problem with authority, rightly or wrongly, and with being told what to do by people I didn't respect. I was a tough guy at Brentwood but not out on the street."

He reckons because he was good at sport – representing Essex at cricket throughout his teenage years – he was tolerated at Brentwood. After obtaining seven GCSEs, however, he was not encouraged to stay on in the sixth form and did his A levels at the somewhat less genteel Havering College.

"My mum dropped me off on the first day and sat in the car crying," Eddie recalls.

After two weeks of not attending classes, he finally went to one when the novelty of not doing anything wore off and noticed just eight of the original 25 students had made it even this far. He asked the teacher why and the answer proved to be a touchstone moment for him.

"He said: 'Well, if people don't want to learn, I can't force them,' and that kick-started me. I went to classes and ended up with an A in media studies and Cs in business studies and PE.

"Dad knew I liked a pound note so he offered me a grand for each A level I got and 10 grand for an A. I got 3 grand. Never did get the 10 grand."

Eddie turned down a place at Bournemouth University and instead went into the sports agency business with a company called BDS. "It was the time of Jerry Maguire," he explains.

After running the sponsorship arm for three years, he moved to the swimmer Duncan Goodhew's management agency LEA and helped recruit and look after golfers and some cricketing figures, including Sir Ian Botham.

A few years later he left to go into the family business and set up a golf arm, joining his sister Katie, two years older, who was running the TV arm of Matchroom after learning the trade as a producer at Sky.

Married with two daughters, Eddie then became Group Managing Director, natural business heir to his father. "Forget the money, my Dad was domineering and powerful in a business sense and instilled an 'us against the world mentality' and a work ethic in me," he says. "I work as hard anyone I know."

He had big success for the company in setting up online and televised poker tournaments, then persuaded his father, who by now had also turned darts into a major attraction, that there was still mileage in the boxing market. Eddie duly set up for Matchroom the Prizefighter series of contests for Sky TV in 2008.

That was supposed to be the extent of the company's involvement in boxing until a chance meeting changed everyone's lives…

"I was in Las Vegas at a poker game when I met Audley Harrison. I told him how surprised I was at how big his profile was when he had been a non-achiever as a pro really. He said he just needed a shot and so I told him about Prizefighter. If he came back to England and won that, he might get a world title shot against David Haye.

I came home and told my old man that I was going to do some work with Audley and he just said: 'Fuck off. You're on your own.' Audley was everything he hated about boxing – fighters trying to control their own promotion. He had got fed up of people like Chris Eubank and Prince Naseem. His motto was fighters fight, promoters promote.

But Audley won Prizefighter and won the European title by beating Michael Sprott and then went on to fight Haye, not that I could be proud of that night. It was an awful fight and Audley froze. I got some stick as a promoter but I believed that he really had been in with a chance. That's Audley all over.

I met Darren as a result of Audley, really. He fought on that Michael Sprott bill and he sold 970 tickets. I was impressed with that. I had a chat with Tony Sims at the weigh-in but it was a while before they came to me, when their contract with Mick Hennessy was up.

Darren was actually the first fighter we officially signed to Matchroom and it opened doors. Kell Brook followed a couple of weeks later, then Carl Froch. Then it became non-stop. After Audley, no matter the result, a lot of fighters saw that I had got him a world title fight. They were ringing to say that if I could do that for him, I must be able to do something for them.

We always pride ourselves on paying people on time and wanted to do things differently. I knew a dozen fighters who had been waiting for money for four months after a fight. It's outrageous. And it was almost like it was the norm. Nobody seemed to complain. When he first started with us, Darren used to ask,

'When will I get paid?' and I said 'Monday.' We always had a poxy little contract with Darren and he could walk away any time but there was no reason for him to.

You can see how people get into trouble. It's a high-risk business and the bigger the arena the higher the risk. You can lose £400,000 on a promotion. My old man fell out of love with boxing because he was dealing with too many arseholes, boxers and families who reckoned they could promote themselves, people who didn't understand the business. He was losing more money, boxers were wanting more money, and he was done.

But I loved the sport. I grew up a boxing nut, reading everything about fighters in the British Boxing Yearbook. I guess we are all in it for the same reason: a little bit of ego, a little bit of money... but mainly the glory. I love it, love the atmosphere round the gyms and the people in it, even if you can be dealing with some iffy characters. If I had sons, I wouldn't hesitate to get them boxing. It teaches them discipline and respect. Nothing gives me so much pleasure or passion. I've been to the tennis at Wimbledon and it bores me.

Anyway, I told Darren that he had to do this properly now. I knew he liked a night out. He was very popular. But we drummed that into him. His next fight, against Domenico Spada, he only sold about 300 tickets personally, but that was because he had got his head down and wasn't out socialising.

We lost about 60 grand on that show. It was one of my first and I wondered what I had got into, but it was a great night and a good atmosphere and we needed to build Darren up again after his injuries and get him that European title.

After that, we were always better off looking for the biggest fight we could get for Darren as we never knew whether he had one fight or five fights left in him. We put our name in the hat for the Martinez fight but it looked as if Matt Macklin was going to get it – even after we had agreed the numbers – because HBO thought Macklin was the sexier fighter. I had to give it the sob story, that Darren really deserved this fight, to get it done in the end. I remember texting him a picture of the contract and he just texted back 'Wow.'

To be honest, I thought Darren was out of his depth at the time. Maybe there was a chance if Martinez proved to be too old or Darren turned out to be better than we thought. In any event, I knew he would not be outclassed and would put up a great fight. Then we could build his profile and get another world title shot.

After the fight, I had never seen swelling on a boxer's face like I did then on Darren's. I could see his family looking worried and I thought 'This is a tough sport.' But he gave a great account of himself and I thought we had momentum.

Then everything folded with the second hip operation, then the torn bicep. It was a total disaster. He came to see me with Tony Sims and said he couldn't fight any more. Every training camp broke his heart, he said. He had no money at the time, hadn't fought for a year. I could see the frustration in him. He was in tears.

I had to say some things I didn't really want to say and outside of how we normally conduct our business. But it would have hurt me if Darren had quit. I remember the conversation. It was on a bench out in the grounds at Mascalls.

I said, 'Let's cut the bullshit. Let's forget the stuff like achieving your dream and becoming a world champion. Let's talk about life and how you are going to provide for your family. Because without boxing you are fucked. What you going to do? Work on a building site? Drive a black cab?'

I remember him saying, 'I take offence at that. I think I can do a lot of things if I put my mind to it.'

I reminded him that he was 29 and had been fighting for more than 15 years and that he once told me he didn't know anything else. 'Tell me where else you can get 30 grand for a night's work?'

What I've always wanted for all my fighters, but especially for Darren, was financial security. When he's 50, I want him to phone me up and I want to go round to his nice house, all paid for, have Sunday lunch and see he's got money in the bank and his kids at a nice school. That's when you can look back and say you did a good job for your fighter.

Darren is a good mate and if I wasn't a promoter he would still be my mate. He was hard work emotionally but I like people who are hard work. You will never find a special fighter who isn't hard work.

He is very ambitious and driven and a true competitor but at the time was caught between the ideas of wanting to win a world title and needing to make money. I told him just to give it another fight. The torn bicep was a freak injury and he would get over it. We could get him a fight for Christmas and see how he was after that.

He took the Kerry Hope fight and surprised himself at how easy it was, I think. He had been working with Chris Kemp on his weights and his physique changed. I'm not sure it was overly beneficial to his boxing but he became stronger and was hitting a lot harder.

I told him we wanted him back in action in a few months and after a bit of grumbling he knuckled down to good effect. He came out a different fighter against Rotolo. Not many people were buying tickets because no-one believed in him any more. But he had a new mentality and it was impressive. He was injury free, getting paid for quick fights and looking good. I thought we could get him another world title fight.

Gennady Golovkin had just won the WBA title and his people phoned up and said they would come to London to defend against Darren for 20 ringside seats and sponsorship of the show, on the ring mat. I couldn't believe it and went to Tony Sims with the deal. He said, 'Fuck off, we're not taking it.' I was gutted about it but Tony knew Golovkin was a monster.

That left Daniel Geale... There were others ahead of Darren but they were pricing themselves out of the market. Darren bit their hand off for the fight. That contract was almost like winning a fight for me. I had done my job in getting it. For Darren it was the defining deal of his career. ”

25

THE FIGHT FOR REDEMPTION

We were walking across the Millennium Bridge, doing what we normally do when celebrating the success of a family member. We were doing it together, the whole lot of us. Mum was in her graduation gown having just been awarded her foundation degree that qualified her to work as a maternity support worker and we were heading from the ceremony on the South Bank into the City for a meal.

My phone rang and Eddie's name came up. I looked at everyone and they all looked back at me expectantly. I paced around a bit before ending the call.

"Well come on. Tell us then," they said.

"It's on," I said. "I've got another world title shot."

They all cheered and we found a pub to have a meal in. We had two things to celebrate now and they all – Dad, Grandad and Nan, Lee, Daisy and Sean – drank to Mum and me. It would be my last pint of lager before the fight. I had been ticking over in the gym but now, from this day in May of 2013, I was in full training for what would be the fight of my life.

We were 14 weeks from the 17th August date set for my challenge to Daniel Geale of Australia for the IBF title. I would be ready.

Sergio Martinez was still bestriding the middleweight world at that time and had just had that win over Martin Murray in the April, but he was now 38 and close to the retirement that would come after he ceded his WBC title to Miguel Cotto in the June.

The pretender to Martinez's undisputed middleweight crown was Gennady Golovkin of Kazakhstan, who had looked fearsome in defeating Matt Macklin that June to retain his WBA and IBO world titles at the Foxwoods Resort in Connecticut, an Indian reservation casino where my fight with Geale was being scheduled. Now Golovkin was setting his sights on other belts...

Geale was in possession of the IBF version and had previously owned the WBA belt, having won it off the tough German of Bosnian extraction, Felix Sturm, the previous September. Geale, though, was controversially stripped of his title by the WBA when he took a big money all-Australian fight for his first defence, against Anthony Mundine, rather than face Golovkin, the mandatory challenger.

Geale was unlucky really. Sturm had been delaying mandatories for a long time but seemed to get away with it. But now the WBA seemed to be fed up with waiting around and ordered Geale to face Golovkin in four and a half months rather than the nine that Sturm was allowed.

Many pundits seemed to think that Geale was the weak link of the various champions but the fact that he had beaten Sturm in Germany and had been the holder of two of the belts surely showed his pedigree. Like me, he had only ever lost one professional fight, his record totalling 30 fights to my 26.

Even so, I fancied my chances. I had grown in confidence after learning so much from being in with the very best in Martinez. Eddie had played a blinder in getting me this fight as though I was now ranked in the top five by the IBF, I was not the mandatory challenger.

It was a good match-up for TV and fight fans too. Geale had won Commonwealth gold at welterweight in Manchester 2002 while I was doing the same at light welterweight, although we had not met then. And this was Great Britain v Australia, the third leg of a sporting trilogy that summer, with the Ashes cricket in England and the Lions Rugby Union team down under.

I was ready for the usual anxieties, aches and pains during my training camp but by now I was a man possessed - and determined to train on and overcome them for this chance. The elbows still gave me pain when it came to sparring time and I was required to throw out some jabs. Over the 14 weeks, I would have four cortisone injections – two in each arm – of those seven I had during my career. They were painful and it was a lot to have but I had to get through the work.

And even after the surgery on both hips, I still had that grinding feeling that meant I was not able to do all the running that I needed to get the endurance for 12 rounds in my legs. As it turned out, though, fortune intervened and I would meet a unique man who could help, another of those people remarkably placed in my path to help me at each stage of my journey.

These days I was regularly using the gym at Chelsea Football Club and earlier in the year, I had run into a bloke called Wayne Leal. Usually, when I was in the zone in the gym, I rarely spoke to people but one day I passed him on the stairs, he said "Hello" and we got chatting.

I told him about my boxing training and mentioned my hip problems. He said he had also had a hip operation and it had led to him adopting different training techniques. Now he used them in his job as a personal trainer. He reckoned I should try them.

And so I did. This was a meeting that was plainly meant to be, and I was intrigued. Each morning during my training for the Geale fight, I would head over there at 7.30 am and he would put me through yoga sessions that would help me centre myself mentally and physically. He also worked on my breathing, believing that if I could control that, I could control my body.

The thinking was that belief in my core strength would give me more belief in my physical condition and thus improve my mental strength. I had always been interested in yoga as I was one of the stiffest, most inflexible of sportsmen and was now finally getting the chance to do it.

In addition, Wayne had me swimming and doing aquarobics to ease the burden on my hips. He also got me working on a mini trampoline rebounder. It meant I still got the fitness work in without having to pound the streets doing so much running or plodding along on a machine. It was perfect for me and I felt the benefits instantly. After that, I would head over to Tony's gym and be ready for an afternoon session of more conventional boxing work.

Wayne and I wound each other up sometimes, mainly because I would whinge about the routine or my aches and pains, but it was a measure of how well and how quickly we got to know each other. We also had a laugh and I suddenly felt a lot stronger physically, which led to an improvement in my mental state as well.

An improved diet helped a lot too. I finally had a better diet regime, thanks to a company called Insight Nutrition who were recommended to me by Tony's brother Peter, and they developed the eating plan for me. It was all worked out for me - how many calories I needed, what amount of rest.

Every day I would cook a steak at 7 am, which sometimes wasn't too popular with Gemma as the smell filled the house, and I also ate plenty of nuts and berries, which I never did before. It was a simple formula: if you stick to this diet, you will lose this amount of weight per week through burning calories.

It was still not easy to stick to the weight programme, as I was always a big middleweight, but I felt better and looked better, with more muscle definition. It helped that I could see the results and that I was so determined now in my training. If ever I got low, I just kept telling myself that I was fighting for a world title in America and that this was the best chance of becoming champion I was ever going to get.

And I was comfortable with the money I was getting, though it wasn't the best. It was a long way short of the purse I received for the Martinez fight, for example, and once all the deductions had come out, such as taxation at source in America and of course all my expenses and Tony's fee, it was not going to be life-changing money.

Still, although I was fighting to get my house finished for Gemma and Scarlett, I was now on a mission, and that world title was all consuming. At this stage of things, I would have fought for nothing, though I would never have told a promoter that. When it came time to head out to America at the start of August, two weeks before the fight, I was ready.

I was delighted that the fight had been switched from Foxwoods to Atlantic City by the HBO TV network and would now take place at the plush new Revel Hotel and Casino at the Northern end of the Boardwalk. I didn't want it out in the sticks, at a place difficult for my fans to get to, being two hours from New York and two from Boston. I wanted redemption in the place where I had lost to Martinez, and for as many people as possible to be there.

The training camp had gone smoothly and I had done plenty different this time but something still had to go wrong. When we flew out, it was with my corner men Peter Sims, Mark Seltzer and my brother and cook Lee. But not Tony. There was some sort of hitch with his visa and it was worrying me that he might not even make it across the Atlantic.

We had an apartment in a nice block in Jersey City, just across the Hudson River from Manhattan and easy to get in to New York itself via the subway, which we often did just to wander through one of the most exciting cities on earth. I was edgy, though, being without my trainer, who was also my mentor and one of my best mates. Tony himself had told me that I just had to get on with it and crack on with my final preparations.

It didn't help when the guy we had lined up for sparring, the Ghanaian Ossie Duran, who had been based in England for a while, didn't show up on the first day at the gym we had booked, about half an hour's drive out into New Jersey. My mood was also not improved when we did an open work-out for the media in New York at the Mendez gym and I got there to find Geale was on first and already at work on the pads.

I thought he looked good and fit and didn't want to see it, so I went out into the street and mooched about until it was my turn. Even then, I didn't enjoy it. I didn't like a gym where all eyes were on me, and this one was packed – as it had been ahead of the Martinez fight. I liked it when lots of other boxers were working out but when I could be more anonymous among them, rather than the centre of attention.

I also had to do some sprinting work to keep up the fitness in the absence of having any access to a pool and I was concerned about my hips. Fortunately we were close enough to fight time and I could just tick over rather than have to push myself, so all was well with my body. And when Ossie eventually turned up, we had some good sessions. He was tough and experienced.

I was always the first out of bed in the morning in the flat, so I was surprised one morning when there was a knock at my bedroom door very early. I was a bit pissed off to be woken up, to be honest. I opened the door bleary-eyed and grouchy but that soon disappeared. There stood Tony, to my shock at first. Then my delight. His visa had finally come through and he had taken an overnight flight, not telling me so as to surprise me and give me a lift. It was fantastic to have him there.

Now I had all my people around me, including the most important one, and I felt that now I was definitely going to win this title. You always stick the hashtag #AndTheNew on the end of your tweets but now I could dare to believe that it was going to be – and meant to be.

My mate Waheed also came out a week ahead of the fight to stay with us and he provided us with some entertainment as well. His hair was thinning on top and we suggested he apply black dye to the bald patch with some foam you could buy. Halfway through the process, he began having doubts and Tony was crying with laughter. Personally, I thought it looked better but I don't think Waheed ever did it again.

It was time, with a few days to go, to move down to Atlantic City. I had a lovely suite at the Revel, which was a high class hotel, striking in appearance with all its black glass, and which had opened only the previous year. They were looking to use boxing to get more business, I was told, and had an events hall inside the building. In fact, because it was high class and so far along the Boardwalk from where the action was in central Atlantic City, it would struggle and close down the following year after just over two years in business.

I loved it, loved being back in town. After the Martinez experience, I felt ready for all the pre-fight atmosphere. My nervousness was more to do with excitement as my family, friends and supporters began to arrive. They were becoming as familiar with the resort as I was. The city was well known for its outlet shops and I think that, collectively, Barnet bought up the Ralph Lauren shop.

The last press conference, two days before the fight, fired me up even more. I felt that the promoter Gary Shaw showed me a lack of respect. He had obviously invested big money in Geale and this promotion to get him better known with an American audience, and so naturally wanted him to shine. He talked about him facing Gennady Golovkin as his next title defence and that annoyed me. What happened to one fight at a time? Anyway, it was me who was going to be doing the defending, I reckoned. Offsetting that, however, was my meeting Roy Jones Junior, who was a boxer I really admired and who was going to be one of the TV commentators.

On the morning of the weigh-in, half an hour before it in fact, I was still a few ounces over, but this time I wasn't worried having been through that experience ahead of the Rotolo weigh-in. I just turned up the heating in the hotel room again, put on a tracksuit and did some shadow boxing.

When it came to the actual weigh-in, I was confident and felt excited as I walked down from my room to the conference room where it was taking place. In fact, I was pretty much bang on – eight ounces under the 160 lbs limit, exactly the same as Geale – and I felt relieved. My barmy army were there again, singing their song about 'There's Only One Darren Barker' and 'Walking in a Barker Wonderland'. It felt good hearing it and Geale's support was heavily outnumbered and certainly outsung.

Now I could relax a bit. Making the weight is always half the battle. In fact I could have a meal in the hotel with the family and some friends and enjoy a hearty portion. I had a steak again. As the golfer Lee Trevino once said: "I like to eat steak. Have you ever seen an unhealthy looking lion?"

Even then I had to be careful, though. You are weighed again the next morning and under the IBF's rules, you have to be no more than 10 lbs over the 160. When my time came to get on the scales, after a good night's sleep, I was just seven pounds over while Geale was at the top end.

That was not a good sign for him, I thought, and I felt encouraged again. I could look forward to a chilled day now ahead of fight night. The pressure was all on him as the champion and the man trying to prove himself to America - having won his title in Europe - if he was to earn the big bucks in the future. I preferred being the underdog.

By now, you will know me a bit better, though. I couldn't go into a world title fight, perhaps a chance I would never get again, without there being some sort of crisis or crises.

26

#ANDTHENEW

Dad could never understand how I could go out and walk for so long on the day of a fight. A short walk in the morning, yes, but he reckoned I should be resting more. I liked and needed the company, though. I enjoyed strolling about with Gemma, and seeing my supporters walking around the Boardwalk and the shopping malls gave me a lift. I also liked raiding the Ralph Lauren outlet before Eddie Hearn bought all the good stuff.

It was when I got back to my room that it hit me. I had been confident throughout the training camp but all of a sudden a wave of self-doubt and negativity overwhelmed me. It was not a good feeling on the day of a fight. It was also an echo of the morning of the Martinez fight, when my head told me I could beat him but my heart felt I wouldn't, though I tried to bury that feeling. Tonight I would either be world champion or - for certain if I lost – my career would be over.

The devil on my shoulder told me it was going to be the second of those two possible outcomes. So many thoughts raced through my head. The fear of losing had always driven me on but it could also drive me mad. I thought about my sessions with Bruce Lloyd, about working through the trauma of Gary's death and being set on what was my intended path to fulfillment.

I thought it would do me good to speak to someone in that way again and rang Wayne Leal, who had made the journey out for the fight. He came to my room and we talked. "This is the chance to write your own book," he said. "Each round will be a new chapter." He also had me meditating, almost hypnotised me in fact, and got me breathing properly again, got me centred. After a couple of hours, the angel on the other shoulder was back. The wise Grandad had taken over from the self-sabotaging kid.

I also took a chance by going on Twitter and running the gauntlet of any trolls but I was gratified to see how much love I was getting. Sky Sports had made a one-hour special documentary about me in the previous few months and had been running it into the build-up to the fight. It had been getting a really good response.

It was a relief that I had snapped out of my down mood and I got myself ready with new enthusiasm, packing my kitbag ready to make the short walk from hotel room to dressing room with Tony and Eddie. Then, just as I was about to leave, somebody knocked on my door. I answered it to find Luke Chandler, my sponsor and good mate.

He just wanted to tell me, he said, what a privilege it had been to share my journey, through all the injuries, all the tough times and adversity that he had witnessed, from me breaking down in Tenerife - physically and emotionally - through the hip operations to this threshold of glory. Whatever happens, he added, I had done him proud. He stood there teary eyed, this big, muscular, tattooed man's man and he almost had me going too. I had been grateful for him being introduced into my life, too.

"Let's do this," he said. I nodded and we hugged. Now it was time. There were three hours till the fight and I wanted to be in my workspace now. I never liked to rush. I went straight to my dressing room rather than to the ring, having visited that the day before with Lee and Waheed. I liked the venue. With a 5,500 capacity, Ovation Hall in the Revel was not as big as Boardwalk Hall but was new and shiny. Intimate. A good place for a world title to change hands.

I have always been a bit of a diva about my dressing rooms and this one was good, like the one at Boardwalk Hall for the Martinez fight, but even more spacious. It had plenty of room to do my shadow boxing and pad work with Tony, was nice and comfortable, with a TV on the white wall and even a sofa.

Although I was not allowed as many visitors as for the Martinez fight, I was allowed visits by the people I wanted in there, mainly my Dad and Grandad. The rituals were observed: the referee – Eddie Cotton again – came to tell me his expectations, Mark Seltzer cut the tape up in his ordered routine and Tony taped my hands with his usual care and attention.

The ring announcer, Michael Buffer, came into the dressing room, though I missed him. I was in the toilet. When I came back, Lee told me he had been winding him up about getting my name wrong at the Martinez fight. It was Barker, not Baker, Lee reminded him and Buffer – everybody in boxing just called him by his surname – apologised. Lee made him say in that familiar drawl of his: "And the new..."

I was getting jittery and ever since that night, when it comes to recalling those moments, the jitters always come back. Especially when it comes to remembering gloving up.

After the weigh-in there is always a rules meeting between the two boxers, if they want to go, their trainers and the local sanctioning body, in this case the New Jersey State Athletic Commission, at which you have to show your gloves to the opponent. I always left it to Tony. At the meeting, he got two pairs of black Lonsdales out of his bag and they were duly authorised.

When I put on a pair now, they just didn't feel right. It was like the stitching of the right hand in the thumb compartment didn't go to the end but cut across, pushing into my thumb. I wondered if I had cut my nails properly. Even though the tape had by now been put on to seal the gloves on my hands and an official had signed them off under the eye of one of Geale's corner men, I told Tony I just couldn't wear them.

He took them off and my thumb really ached. Then we had to get the representative of the British Boxing Board of Control present with us to go and get the other gloves we had lodged with the Athletic Commission. When I put those on, they were even worse. Now the left hand was all wrong. Time was ticking by and Eddie and Tony were getting twitchy, as were my corner men, Mark and Peter Sims.

We took those gloves off and put the others back on but I was unnerved and unhappy as I did my shadow boxing then hit the pads with Tony. I always did have a touch of OCD when it came to my gloves. All this as officials and Geale's camp observed and waited.

The call came. It was time. TV was ready for us. There was nothing I could do about it any more. I would just have to hope that in the rush of all the adrenaline, I would forget about the gloves. As I walked to the ring, the cheers in my ears and my music playing, luckily I did. I could hear just before my entrance Michael Buffer announcing my name right this time – 'Dazzling Darren Barker'. With an r.

Having heard it on that Sky Sports documentary about me, I chose 'I Still Haven't Found What I'm Looking For' by U2 as my ring walk tune, in conjunction with my self-appointed musical director, Luke Chandler. I liked a couple of the verses that seemed appropriate for me, and the chorus that summed up my motivation…

I spoke with the tongue of angels,
I have held the hand of a devil,
It was warm in the night,
I was cold as a stone.

I believe in the Kingdom Come,
Then all the colors will bleed into one.

Bleed into one.
But, yes, I'm still running.

But I still haven't found,
What I'm looking for…

I completed my ritual once in the ring of bouncing off all four sets of ropes but that done, it felt like a long wait until the formalities were over. The worst thing about being the challenger is that you have to endure the champion's own ring walk for what seems like an age. It is all part of the showbusiness of a major fight but it can be intimidating and tonight it was, as Geale had a didgeridoo player blowing that Australian aborigine horn as loud as he could.

It went on for a while, too, before he was in the ring. Funny, back in 2002, he had been the next fight on after me at the Commonwealth Games and we had also boxed in other amateur tournaments but never met or fought against each other. Now here we were in the same square space ready to face off. Now Buffer was launching his trademark announcement: "LET'S GET READY TO RUMBLE..."

The game plan was to box in a more controlled way than I had in the Hope and Rotolo fights. Tony was always a big fan of my technical ability that had been honed at Repton and wanted me to be smart and intelligent, to overpower Geale with combinations we had worked on that we thought would get through his defence. The combos would be fast, two bursts of four punches, and I would follow up my work and hold the centre of the ring.

Tony wanted me to be aggressive but not gung ho, more on the front foot than in the Martinez fight, as I was the bigger and stronger boxer. I had watched videos of Geale and thought I could get through his guard and take him at close quarters.

When that bells sounds, though, and theory becomes practice, only then do you really know what you are up against. And immediately I could see why people were wrong to underrate him. He was awkward, as he bounced and bobbed, and every time I thought I had landed a shot, he would be just a millimetre out of range.

I had to adapt quickly and I actually managed to catch him in the first round with a left hook that sent him back on the ropes. I knew I had hurt him and it gave me encouragement to go for him in the second. I also remembered the lessons from the Martinez fight, when he impressed the judges with late attacks, and so an overhand right to the head and a body shot just before the bell gave me the round, I reckoned, after an even opening one. By now, the dodgy gloves had gone right out of my mind.

It was the fittest I had ever been and while Tony was telling me between rounds to get back to my boxing a bit more, he wasn't worried. He reckoned I was winning the rounds. I thought there was not much in it but that I was up after five rounds. The statistics would later show that I landed more punches in the third and fourth rounds, 24-18 and 22-8.

He came back strongly in the fifth as we traded punches evenly in what was becoming an intense fight and he might just have shaded that one, inflicting the only significant cut of my career, above my left eye, but I reckoned I was at least two rounds up. Tony said it was all going to plan, that I was now in control of the fight, even if I had had to modify the strategy, what with Geale being so awkward.

Then came the sixth, the most epic round of boxing I would ever be involved in. It would be the moment that defined my career and probably said the most about me as a human being, or would say about me for the rest of my life.

The round was meandering. We were mid fight and both getting our second wind, both of us probably settling in for the long haul. Or so I thought. I tried a few body shots to slow him down but all of a sudden it was him catching me, and with a humdinger.

It went flush into my rib cage. At first, I thought it had sunk deep into my solar plexus but the pain was in the ribs.

It was funny. Before fights, once I had the gloves on, I used to hit myself on the jaw and the body just to feel the force of a punch, to get myself going. Tonight, I had hit myself in the rib cage and felt a pain. I remembered thinking then that I hoped I didn't get hit there. But that was exactly where I had just got hit.

I had been winded before but this was something different altogether, a mix of agony and breathlessness. I went down on the canvas like a roll of carpet.

People have asked me many times since about the nine and a half seconds I spent down there and how I got up. In the early days and months after the fight, I simply shrugged my shoulders, unsure myself, before smiling and thanking fate. Even today there is still an element of mystery. But I have thought about it a lot as time has gone by. So, this is how. And why.

Normally when I fought, all I could hear was a muffled, indistinct crowd noise. The only voices I could ever pick out were Tony, my Dad and my Grandad - the people closest to me who had been there down all these years of my boxing. Right now, though, all I could hear was a ringing in my ears.

I was kicking my feet on the canvas as I was in so much pain. I could feel myself breathing, gasping for breath. It's always said that when people are dying, their whole life flashes in front of them. That's how it was. I was down for nine and a half seconds. But it felt like a lifetime.

My brother's face flashed in front of me. Then my daughter's. I can't say categorically that Gary was telling me to get up but strong forces were definitely at work. I certainly sensed his spirit. I knew what I really wanted and what was important to me. I knew I was doing this for all the right reasons. The promise I had made to my brother in the past. The desire to provide for my daughter in the future.

Those twin sentiments and motivations overrode the pain. Come on. Get up, Darren. Fuck it. I suppose a bit of the fear of humiliation came into it too. Boxers hate being knocked down by a body punch then counted out. It's not like being hit round the head is it? Actually, it can be worse...

Then it became like you would imagine in a boxing movie. The slow motion scene suddenly became normal speed again. The ringing turned into a huge wall of noise in the arena. I was suddenly able to make a conscious decision and that decision was simply to get up. I guess I must have been aware of the referee counting, maybe hearing the numbers subconsciously, but it didn't feel like it. I was operating on instinct.

Suddenly ref Eddie Cotton was in my face asking if I was OK. I still couldn't breathe properly, was trying to take in gulps of air, but told him I was. It seemed to work and he was ready to let me box on. I suppose I would have accepted it if he had stopped it, as boxers do, by and large, with refereeing decisions because it is a sport that teaches you respect, but I would have been furious.

Now I was in survival mode and while Geale's corner were shouting at him to go in for the kill, telling him that I had gone, I felt strangely good. 'Right,' I said to myself. 'You've done the hard bit... You're up now... Might as well keep going... At least you haven't gone out on the floor... Survive, survive, survive…'

I bit into my gumshield and came to my senses. I held him off then started throwing a few punches. They were landing. I was back in the game. And when I heard the clapper that signalled the last 10 seconds, I felt better, no longer winded. I reckoned I had won a battle, a battle with myself, and proved that I was a tough man, resolute and durable, which I always wanted to do. That was a great glory in itself.

I even raised my arms aloft as the bell sounded. I was not being cocky but I sensed a power shift and I wanted Geale to see that I was indomitable. I knew he had won the round 10-8 due to the knockdown but I had sent a message to him and his corner. He must have wondered what he had to do to get rid of me. I wondered what he had to do to get rid of me. I hoped he felt dispirited. I certainly felt galvanised.

When I got back to the corner, Tony asked me if I was all right now. I apologised to him for getting caught with the shot. I don't know why I apologised. I was still feeling tender in the rib cage but I was now ready to go back to the game plan. I listened to him now for his specific instructions, to box my way back into my rhythm. He told me that although I may have lost the round, I was still winning the fight.

I trusted him implicitly. Through shared experience, we were in sync. I was like an iPhone plugged into a Mac computer.

In the seventh, I re-established my authority, landing an uppercut with about a minute left, then another right just before the bell. I boxed really nicely, I felt, to win it. In fact it was beautiful. The best round of the fight for me, especially given what I had been through in the previous three minutes.

From then on, the rounds seemed so long, like two or three rounds' worth, so intense were they. The minutes between them, in contrast, felt like seconds. No sooner was I slumping on the stool than I was up off it again.

Later, I would come to see that the fight had everything and would be a contender for fight of the year. Technically and tactically it was of a high standard and it also had heart and soul. It was, in hindsight, a privilege to be part of it. Not that I was having any thoughts like that at the time. Boxing is great for keeping you living in the moment. Except when you are down for nine and half seconds, it seems..

Here, now, it was simply about matching him. It was so draining and demanding, physically and mentally, that I couldn't switch off for a second. I knew I would have been down again if I had. He was 100 miles an hour.

I had him again in the eighth and caught him with another combination late in the round, two jabs and a hook, followed by a left to the body. In the ninth, though I took a good right hand, I thought I made it three rounds in a row thanks to more solid combination punching of the sort I had been working on in sparring.

In the 10th, he came at me with more body shots again, as if trying to recapture what he had achieved in the sixth, but I was a different fighter to then. I knew I was on the cusp of my destiny and I was ready for it now. He was battling hard, and he was proving to be a great opponent, but I thought my harder punching won me the 11th as well.

It came to the 12th and I knew it was close. Eddie would later tell me that he was shouting from ringside: "You've got to win this one, Daz." I was in a cocoon by now though. And I also genuinely felt I had the edge. His corner were telling him he was winning, I heard when I later came to see footage, but I reckon it was just bravado and Geale knew the real score. Which was why he came out strong and caught me a couple of times, though I responded in kind and was going down no more.

I was just thinking that if I could sustain a good round, I would clinch it. I kept working and moving and throwing punches. When it came to the last 10 or 15 seconds, I raised my arms because I was convinced I had done enough to win. Any fighter, amateur or professional, knows when they have done enough. What you don't know is which way the verdict might go. This was his promoter's show and I was the away fighter. I knew I was proud of myself, though. I had toughed it out in the toughest of adversity.

Tony towelled me down, told me he was proud of me as well and we waited for the judges' scorecards. Eddie climbed into the ring and said it could go either way. It could even be a draw, meaning Geale would retain his title.

As I prowled for what seemed an age, I took stock: I had come to Atlantic City and heard the final bell. I had gone the distance, literally and metaphorically, and left everything in the ring against a two-time world middleweight champion.

The stats would show that I had thrown 862 punches to Geale's 693, 582 of them power punches compared to his 503. That's why you work on the heavy bag. I had also connected with more punches, 292 to 259. All that without doing any running, just swimming and yoga. Mad.

Suddenly Buffer is in the ring with the scorecards and the bell is ringing to say that we have a result from the three judges, all of them American. The first comes out for Geale, 114 to 113, from Alan Rubenstein of Pennsylvania and I think that I can't possibly win from here. But hold on. The second is for me, 116 to 111, from Barbara Perez of New Jersey. That's decent. Convincing. We are level going to the final card.

What I didn't see was my brother Lee at ringside. He had seen the judges' cards and knew the result, was trying to let me know, then turning round to tell my family at ringside.

Then Buffer announces that it is 114 to 113 on the final card, that of Carlos Ortiz of New York. We have a winner, I thought. It's definitely not a draw. And then I hear the words coming out of his mouth, his voice rising in volume: "AND THE NEW…" This time he wasn't practising it in a dressing room. This time it was for real.

I was delirious. I leapt into the air. I ran to the ropes in delight, Tony trying to grab me. After that, I fell to the canvas in disbelief, holding my head in my gloves, and all I heard was Tony shouting: "Get up, Darren Barker, you're the champion of the world."

Emotion overwhelmed me. Eddie was in tears too. I think I hugged everyone I could find. Dad came to the ring, Grandad and Gemma too. In their excitement, some friends actually jumped in it, including Lee Waite and Wayne Leal. They got led out.

There was just one person missing and in my interview with Max Kellerman of HBO, I dedicated this crowning moment to him. Yes, my mad, beautiful kid brother. Gary, I reckoned, would almost certainly have been a world champion. We definitely had one in the family now.

As for my other brother, I was just glad Tony had calmed him down during the fight. At the press conference – sunglasses covering my swollen, cut eyes – I was asked about a rumpus in my corner at a point in the fight when I was under the cosh. I only found out about it afterwards. I took a sip of water and coughed as it slipped down the wrong way but everyone thought I was referring to what happened with Lee and starting laughing.

It turned out that Lee had urged Tony to throw in the towel when I staggered to my feet in that sixth round but Tony had told him to calm down. He didn't, though, and instead grabbed the towel. Tony had to take it off him, telling him not to do that ever again. Lee was glad he never did throw it. But having been Lee Purdy's trainer for a night, I knew how tough the moment was. And Lee was family, loved me and was looking out for me, so I know doubly what he was going through.

After all the media obligations, which to be fair Geale fulfilled graciously despite being thwarted in keeping his title by just half a second, and in which Gary Shaw redeemed himself by congratulating me, we went up to a nice private bar at the Revel. This time, I wasn't asked for ID - but then Barry Hearn was sorting out Champagne all round. Everyone was there – the family and my boxing family: Eddie, Luke and Lee Purdy, Martin Ward and Ryan Taylor from our gym. Rob McCracken, Tony's great mate and fellow trainer, was also there. It was a great night.

We discussed the result and the three judges' verdicts. Rubenstein had Geale ahead by two rounds going into the last and I was comfortably ahead on the Perez card at the start of the 12th. That meant it had come down to Ortiz's card. He had it at 104-104 going into the last round. And he gave that to me. That's how close it was. One round in the end.

Even as a world champion – how great did that sound? – I just couldn't party all night given the toll the fight had taken from me and wanted my bed. But I would doze in and out of sleep for just a couple of hours, just about recalling an early morning phone call congratulating me from Colin Hart, the great boxing writer of *The Sun*.

I then went down to the huge breakfast buffet laid on for the staff of the Revel and for which I had a pass. I managed to get pretty much everyone I knew in there and half of Barnet were eating like kings. No wonder the hotel went bust. Somebody managed to find Grandad, who had gone missing. He was asleep on a wall outside the front of the hotel.

From there it was back to New York City in a limo with the fight being played on a TV screen. The first time I saw it, I could not believe I had got up in that sixth round. Back in New York, it was on to the Hard Rock Cafe, where a dozen of us took up residence for the day and evening, me with battered face still wearing the sunglasses. I ate and ate. And drank a few beers, I have to admit.

I thought I would have a hangover when I woke up in our hotel room on the Monday morning but it was not my head that was aching. My body was in bits from my forehead to my nose to my ears to my jaw to my torso to my arms to my hands to my legs to my feet. Not a square inch of me was free from pain. I had never felt like that after any previous fight – and that included Martinez.

Gemma's response was typically down to earth. We were going shopping in Manhattan and I was bag carrier. The respect you get as a world champion, eh?

27

LOOK GAL…

The view across Central London was gorgeous this sunny summer's morning as I gazed out from the top floor of the Lillywhite's building in Piccadilly and I could not have felt happier. It was a natural and literal high. Look Gal, top of the world.

We had just flown back from New York – me, Gemma, Daisy and Sean, and in economy; I wasn't made of money yet – and I had gone straight from Heathrow to the famous London sports shop, to the boxing department at the top, to fulfill a commitment to one of my sponsors, Lonsdale, and pose for the photographers. I didn't look at my best, though, with my eyes still black and swollen, but I didn't care.

I was a proud Londoner back in my city as a world champion, though not with the IBF world title belt. I had been awarded it after the fight but got to keep it only for the press conference and the photos. After that it went back to Daniel Geale to keep. Another one would be made for me and in a few weeks time, Eddie would be texting me a picture of it and I would go over to the Matchroom HQ to pick it up in its presentation box and tissue paper and hand over to Dad for his collection.

The day after getting back from America, suited and booted, it was down to Stamford Bridge to parade in front of my fellow Chelsea fans ahead of the match against Aston Villa, with the IBF International belt I had won for beating Simone Rotolo being used as the stand-in. What mattered to me most was finally getting on to the pitch. It was wonderful taking the applause from around the ground and it was another good night as we won 2-1.

It was all part of a whirlwind initiation as world champion, a status that opens all sorts of doors for you. I went from studio to studio doing TV, radio and press interviews and making personal appearances. From being a reasonably well known British boxer, I was now being recognised by people other than fight fans. I loved it.

I also loved a night out with Joe Calzaghe and walking towards his house in West London to meet him one night shortly after getting back from Atlantic City, he came out of his front door and walked up the street to meet me. "And the New..." he shouted when he got near me. "I told you, didn't I?" he said with a big smile, reminding me of that time I had been down and thinking of quitting when needing the first hip operation when he urged me to carry on because he knew I could be world champion. I could only smile back.

After the media exposure, some nights out and a short holiday with Gemma and Scarlett in Portugal at the Hearn family villa, it was quickly back to work, though. I was always the type who liked to enjoy himself between fights and I didn't want that to get out of hand so I reckoned it was best if I got back into action as soon as possible. As a world champion now, I had a responsibility to the title, to stay in shape. Now was the time to cash in as well, to be honest, with a lucrative first defence as soon as possible.

There were all sorts of things going on with me. For a start, I didn't know how long my body was going to hold up, so I needed to make hay while the sun was shining. As a champion, you are inevitably going to be paid a lot more than a challenger, so the chance was opening up to make my family secure for a long time.

Even before the Geale fight, Eddie had been talking to the representatives of Felix Sturm, from whom Geale had taken the title, and who was the IBF's mandatory challenger. I'm sure Geale's people were doing the same. Sturm had a big TV deal in Germany and his camp were starting to talk Teutonic telephone numbers for us to go over there.

Before that could happen, though, there was a massive and worrying scare that could have seen me stripped of the title and any deal scuppered before the negotiations even got going properly.

Geale's camp had decided to appeal the result of our fight and lodged a protest with the IBF. They cited a host of what they saw were anomalies. First, they said Eddie Cotton, the referee, was slow to start the count when I hit the canvas. They reckoned if you started the count from then to when I got up, it was 11.1 seconds.

They added that I had not got up properly when the ref waved his hands to indicate, according to them, that the fight was over before changing his mind – again, so they said – and allowing it to continue. They were also questioning the scoring in some of the rounds but mainly the decisive 12th.

It was a strange situation for Matchroom, I know that. Geale's promoter Gary Shaw was now a co-partner with Eddie for my next fight, as that was in the contract for my next fight, should I beat his man, as I did. There was also a rematch clasue for further down the line. And here he was trying to get one over his co-partner. It was not going to make things easy.

Eddie had to fly back out to Atlantic City for an IBF hearing, which could have declared it a no contest, overturned the decision, or could have ordered a rematch on poor financial terms for me. I was worried and so was Eddie.

He told me that in the hearing, they replayed the sixth round three times and examined Eddie Cotton's role in it. Then they watched the 12th round as many times.

Eddie pleaded my case, saying that it always takes time for a referee to get a boxer into a neutral corner before he begins a count. He insisted the footage did not show the referee crossing his hands to signal the end of the contest as he reached the count of nine, although he had raised them in preparation as I was getting up. I had got up before he could cross them and say '10.'

And to counter Geale's people's assertion that their man had done more work and pushed me back in the 12th, Eddie pointed out that that was simply their opinion. Two of the three judges had given the round to me and they were the ones whose opinion mattered more as they were independent.

Eddie flew home not knowing the verdict and it was an anxious time. We didn't get the email with the verdict of the commission until five days later . Geale's camp had no case, it said. Darren Barker remained the champion.

It was a huge relief and now Eddie could get on with making the match with Sturm. We looked at trying to get him to Wembley Arena but his people made it plain he was a homeboy and that he was never going to fight outside Germany. Nearly 10 years earlier, he had lost a decision in Las Vegas to Oscar de la Hoya that was highly questionable and had never since left his home country to fight.

If we couldn't agree a deal to go to Germany, the fight would go to purse bids and Sturm's people would pull their fighter out. That would mean no big money defence.

We knew that the real money was in going over there. A Wembley Arena fight would certainly generate good money for me but when the figures were laid out for me, I would be getting around three times what I could get for fighting in London. The money would be enough to pay off my mortgage and then have enough over to invest in my family's future.

I told Eddie to take the deal. There were two simple criteria: I wanted to fight the best and get the most money possible for it. I didn't know how long my body would last. This way I could get in one fight what three defences at home would take me to earn.

Besides, I was supremely confident I could take Sturm, no matter where the fight took place. I thought his style was made for me, that I was better in every department, from movement to punching power.

My ratonale also took in the fact that I had won the title abroad so why couldn't I defend it abroad? I could make my money, then if all went as I expected, have a homecoming in England with a more comfortable, even if less lucrative, fight for the fans back home as a second defence.

The match was made for the Porsche Arena in Stuttgart on December 7th 2013, three days before the seventh anniversary of Gary's death. I was OK with that. I was used to fighting around that date and it was another reminder of why I was doing this, as a way of his name being remembered too.

At a press conference in mid-October to announce the fight formally in London, I said: "I've boxed all over the world as an amateur, in some pretty hostile places, and it's never bothered me. It inspires me. I don't worry about the judges. I plan on winning very well, and putting on a fantastic night with lots of my fans coming over for a great fight between two great champions."

It was pretty much the same thing I had said the day before when I had flown to Stuttgart for a press conference there. But a boxer never really knows until he gets back into a full training camp and has to grind it out all over again how he is going to feel and whether he is going to have the same hunger. Somebody once said that it is harder to defend a title than win it and I would certainly come to agree with that.

In fact, I am honest enough to say that, yes, some of the desire had gone from me when I got back in the gym. I had just been so focused on Geale, so mentally and physically driven, that I was going to beat pretty much anyone put in front of me at that time. Including Sturm. Now it was tougher going through it all again. I was a different animal and the buzz of the Geale camp deserted me. I would have to conjure up new motivation.

I was still determined to do it and to retain my title. Tony was on my case in the gym all the time and we both insisted I was not going out there to lose. I had worked so hard for the title and my journey had been such a long one that I was not about to let it go lightly. I was still sure that my fierce, stubborn competitive nature would see me through, coupled with my confidence about being a far better boxer than Sturm.

And naturally I wanted to respect the title. It was not only about staying in shape but about an attitude as well. Being world champion brought a duty and a dignity, a responsibility both to the sport and its fans.

I had to keep so many things secret during that camp and in the build-up of the last week or two, however, so badly was my body creaking again. I didn't want Sturm and his camp to know that I was struggling. In fact, I didn't want anyone to know, sometimes not even Tony. I didn't want to put the fight in any doubt and I still retained the dogged belief that I could take him. I was not going to offer any excuses.

I worked again with Wayne Leal, doing all the yoga and swimming, and being in the water continued to help my hips so that I could do some stamina work without pain. I also did more of the work on the mini rebounder trampoline, to cut out the impact on the joints, that I had done ahead of the Geale fight.

Now even that hurt, though, as I worked on my movement and bounced up and down. It worsened as the weeks went on. I couldn't even slip in the odd hill sprint that I had got away with ahead of Geale.

And when it came to sparring, my mobility was lacking, worryingly. I was up for it all, got back in my gym bubble and was pre-occupied all the time with the fight, still on the Insight diet plan and doing all right with the weight, but it wasn't always the actual boxing on my mind. The injuries were taking over.

A new thought came to me. I began to worry about something happening that might make me miss out on the biggest payday of my career. I wanted to protect myself, to wrap myself in cotton wool, but it was impossible. Training is physical. You've got to get the fitness work in and do the practice rounds.

At first it was fine, though I did have a scare during some rounds with the talented Anthony Ogogo when he bloodied my nose. Seeing the blood, I got anxious that my nose might be broken, having seen it before with Martinez, and imagined my fortune going up in smoke, so I pulled out. It was wise but it showed just how vulnerable I felt.

Then, a month before the fight, the pain in my right hip became a serious problem, not that I dared confide in anyone about it.

Tony and I had agreed a simple fight plan. Actually, even if we hadn't agreed it and it had been Tony's plan, I would have gone along with it because I trusted him so much.

The idea was to be elusive and move in and out of contact with Sturm, who boxed on the front foot. I was to come forward, and to score and get out of there. To stick to the pedigree boxing I had learned at Repton. If that didn't work, I could always use my size and strength to overcome him as a plan B.

For the next two weeks, though, I was just standing toe to toe in sparring, fighting like Sturm did - having wars. It wasn't me. Tony was telling me to move, asking me what I was doing – or not doing. One day, I threw an uppercut off the back foot and it turned my hip. It was agony but I made out to Tony that the problem was with my elbow. I could get away with that because my elbows were often still a problem and I had another cortisone injection during this training camp.

I knew the hip problem was serious but I told Tony I would be fine. My performances in the ring remained lack-lustre, though, and a fortnight before the fight, he took me into his office.

"What's going on, Daz?" he asked me.

I had to come clean about the hip and I begged him not to pull me out of the fight. I told him that I thought I could still win.

We talked it over, taking into account the money, the title and my health, which was not great but good enough for me to hold on to my title, I insisted. Then we considered all the fans who had booked travel, hotels and tickets. We discussed all the TV arrangements and media commitments.

A decision had to be made. Tony talked about pulling me out and rescheduling but I just wanted to get on with it now, having got this far. Besides, if we rescheduled, would my body be any better? I was never going to be 100 per cent again, given what was going on with me. And anyway, if something was going to go wrong, it could still go wrong on the first day of the next training camp.

I certainly didn't want to go out having conceded my title without even fighting, by withdrawing and being unable to defend and two fighters contest a vacant IBF world championship. I also thought that if I did withdraw, people would think I had bottled it. I told Tony to give me this chance, that I knew I could still win. He was concerned for me because he had my welfare at heart, and a duty of care towards me, but he could see how determined I was and he agreed.

And so we went ahead and flew out to Germany to make final preparations. Unhappily, things did not get any better during the final days, however.

Because I had not been able to train properly, the weight was now harder to shift and two days before the fight, I was still three pounds over. I went back to turning the heat up in my room in our hotel just outside Stuttgart and shadow boxing in the well equipped gym they had there to sweat it off. In the end, I would make the weight fine, at 159 lbs and 9 ozs to Sturm's 159 lbs 3 ozs.

On top of all these worries, every time I threw a right hand on the pads with Tony, my elbow was pinching. I tried not to wince so as to keep it from Tony, which wasn't right. He was my trainer, my mentor, and it showed just how much I wanted this fight to go on that I still wasn't wanting to acknowledge my true vulnerability. I should have done, I suppose. But we had had the conversation already a couple of weeks earlier. I had gone too far and it was too late to stop now.

I was in a worse mood than normal before a fight. The lack of food always made me ratty and the meals that were little and often a couple of weeks before were now down to just little. It would be a bowl of porridge in the morning or a slice of toast, then chicken or fish with salad for a main meal but they were tiny portions of just a few mouthfuls.

I remember having to do a photoshoot the day before the fight after the weigh-in and I was getting really agitated with the photographer in the chilly December air. I was worried about getting a cold or flu that might debilitate me or even halt the fight.

From a feeling of having the world at my feet a few months ago, I now felt I had it on my shoulders.

28

THE FINAL BELL

It took me 18 months to watch the footage of my last professional fight, so painful was it to contemplate and recall. I tried to feel it all, tried to believe that it would be all right on the night and to believe in myself, but this time it all felt so different. Looking back, so much was wrong, however much I tried to mask it.

Take, for example, that ritual of mine to get a feel for a venue – arriving early and, before it filled up, going into the hall, walking around then climbing up into the ring, like in Rocky – which had served me well for 27 professional fights. With my world championship contests, I even liked to do it the day before.

For my 28th and third world title fight, though, I went straight to the dressing room at the 8,000-capacity Porsche Arena that would later be filled to the rafters. I just had no desire to go into the arena, either the day before or on the night, and didn't really know why.

Perhaps I knew it was going to be bigger and more hostile than it was for my last fight in Atlantic City at Ovation Hall, where I had better support than Geale, so didn't want to be in my dressing room imagining it filling up with German fans in the hours leading up to my ring walk. It might also have had something to do with my wanting to get in and get out with my title as quickly as possible, without any fuss.

Despite all the setbacks in the build-up to the fight, I felt confident. Or at least confident enough to win. There was a good buzz in my dressing room, with all my family again allowed in to wish me well. Joe Calzaghe also called in. I was eager now to get out there and get the job done. I went through my routine of Tony taping my hands then doing my pad work and shadow boxing, placing my faith in my old default position - that the adrenaline produced by the first bell would carry me through all my physical deficiencies.

I may have struggled to recapture my hunger for boxing once I had become world champion but now I was here, I was in my zone and I knew I was capable of winning. No doubt about it, Sturm was a good fighter - in my opinion the victim of a bad decision in that Oscar De La Hoya fight in Vegas - but I was convinced I had more in my armory, even if I was going into a hostile atmosphere, similar to Sturm in the United States. Matt Macklin, after all, had boxed really well against Sturm in his title challenge and many good judges had him winning but not getting the points decision.

My ring walk was to a dance tune of the time, Look Right Through by Storm Queen. But funky as it was and as loud as they played it, it was hard to make out the music amid the din of the German supporters whistling and jeering me as it struck up. When I began my walk, my first glimpse of the hall revealed the most intimidating atmosphere I had ever been thrust into. I had heard boos from the Argentinians in the crowd when I fought Martinez but this was on a different planet.

My crowd are normally loud themselves but they were drowned out. It didn't help that there was flight trouble back in England at Gatwick Airport and some of them hadn't made it. And I had never known so many spotlights swirling around a place. It was like the fireworks at Disney World.

After getting my senses back, I buzzed off this hostile atmosphere, though, wanting to embrace it. I always wanted to experience everything in boxing and this was a new side to it for me. I had had so much love in recent years from the British public but now it was almost fun being the bad guy for a change. One routine I did observe fully was to bounce off the ropes on all four sides of the ring to mark my territory. I was ready now.

The only louder noise than the jeers for me were the cheers for Sturm I had heard from the corridor outside my dressing room – as champion, I got to follow him into the ring. His ring walk was to Bleed It Out by Linkin Park, with it's pounding lyric of "Bleed it out, digging deeper, just to throw it away." The volume was cranked right up and the atmosphere was electric.

I knew I had to block out all the sound and fury and concentrate on what this was – a contest between two boxers. And, comparing and contrasting, I still believed I was the better one. The ring, I remembered again, is always the same size no matter whether it's an empty gym, small hall or vast arena. And in football they have a saying: play the game not the occasion.

Sturm's style was very economical and he had a tight guard. He was not especially quick on his feet, though had decent footwork, and his hand speed was not lightning quick. Like me, he was a big strong middleweight, if not as big as me. Apart from possibly his guard, I thought I was better in every department, though. I had better punching power due to my hand speed, was quicker and more nimble.

At least I should have been. When the first bell sounded, I immersed myself in the job and felt OK but as I tried to jab and move, a pain shot through my right hip. Very quickly I found myself back deep in the limitations that had spoilt my sparring and I was having to stand there slugging it out. It was all wrong again. It was just not my style.

I did land one uppercut and I know I hurt him as he took a step back, which he never usually does. It hurt me too, though. After that, every time I threw a right hand, I couldn't get full power into it as I couldn't move properly. I didn't trust my body and I worried about it buckling. With good reason, it would turn out.

I made it to the end of the round, which he had probably just shaded, though I did work hard in the late stages to try and catch the judges' eyes, and I told Tony about the hip. He told me to give it another round and see how it went. I was determined to go on, hoping I might catch Sturm with a good shot for a stoppage or even a knock out.

But after I'd launched a flurry of attacking punches, it was me that got caught early in the second. The hook to my temple went straight to my legs, which gave way, and I hit the floor. I was in agony now with my hip but gave it one more go. I was never a quitter. A minute had gone and another would pass with me doing all right but then I got caught again and my legs buckled badly. On the canvas, I could see my right leg at an awkward angle and I looked towards Tony and shook my head.

I wasn't going out on the floor so I got up once more and tried to box on. My legs were wobbling, though. But after taking a look for around another 15 seconds, Tony decided it was time to throw in the towel, with just under a minute to go in the round. I threw up my arms in frustration, wanting to fight on but unable to, and I knew in my heart Tony that had made the right decision.

After the formalities of him being announced the winner, I limped back to my dressing room and sat down. That was when the pain really kicked in, without the anaesthetic of the adrenaline. Whereas it had been a series of stabbing pains that I had tried to work through, now it was nagging. It was agony.

Early reports suggested I had dislocated my hip but that would have been a bit too dramatic and I would not have been able to walk if that had been true. Even so, it was nasty enough. The hip may not have come out of the socket but the bone was certainly jarring against the inside of it once more.

It ached like hell – would do for days – and a doctor who came into the dressing room suggested I should go to hospital. I had no desire to sit around for hours while they did all sorts of X-rays, tests and examinations, though. I just wanted to go back to my hotel room and hide away in my shame, then get home as soon as possible the next day.

It would be another a couple of hours before I could leave the dressing room, though and I had to ask Eddie to do the press conference on my behalf. Apart from not being able to face it, I just could not give a sample for the drug tester, despite drinking litres of water. I was that dehydrated.

Drug testing for boxers, by the way, is compulsory either before or after a title fight – it was before against Martinez and after against Geale – and I was also tested at least once randomly during a training camp. They could come to your home early in the morning if they wanted, as they did for all three of my world title fights, in the later stages of my camp.

I had no problem with that and I think there should be more of it. I detest cheats in any sport and especially my own and anything that can be done to weed them out is fine by me.

In Europe, the system is stringent, with the tester even following you to the toilet to make sure it is your urine and you are not switching it. In America, it was less rigorous around my title fights and they would wait while you went off into the toilet. You could certainly have switched samples there if you were of that mind.

On title fight nights, you could be tested either before or after a fight and I preferred before, for reasons that were apparent as I hung about in the dressing room with midnight approaching. As I waited to provide a sample, I had a quiet moment with Tony.

"That's it now, Tone," I said. "That's me done."

"Yeah, I know," he said. There was nothing more to be said between us. Our journey together as fighter and trainer, with a bond as tight as you could get, was over. My body had reached the end of the road and my mind knew it.

When Dad arrived, I told him the same thing. I just wanted to tell the two people who had been closest to me in my boxing career first. It felt good to hear myself saying it. A massive relief.

Eddie had been clever and negotiated a rematch clause and he persuaded me not to make any hasty decisions, just to enjoy Christmas and the New Year then if I still felt the same way once the dust had settled, we could make any announcement in January. I agreed but I knew I was not going to change my mind.

Eddie apparently said to Tony that he was gutted for me, but Tony said not to be because of my relief, so he soon cheered up. Eddie would later say to people that my dressing room after the fight was the least disappointed loser's dressing room he had ever seen.

It wasn't that I was not disappointed. In fact, I was devastated by the way it had ended, with me unable to do myself justice on the night. It was just that relief was the overriding emotion. I wouldn't have to go through all the privations of making the weight any more and would no longer have to make demands on this aching body that was betraying me. Along with relief, I had my release from it all.

In the immediate aftermath, I would get stick in some quarters, mainly from some trolls on Twitter, for taking the fight when I knew I was in a bad state, and for going abroad for the money, but I would like them to have walked a mile in my shoes with the offer as it was and my belief that even with my limitations I could still win. I didn't want to get into online rows with anyone so I just left Luke Chandler to reply and explain on my behalf what I had been through until I was ready to engage with them again.

Sturm was hungry that night as it was the last fight of his TV deal and he needed a big performance. He also wanted to make history by becoming the first four-time German world champion. No doubt the better fighter on the night won. But I maintain that a fit Darren Barker in the frame of mind that took on Daniel Geale, confident because he could rely on his body, would have beaten a fit Felix Sturm. I know I was in a different class.

When I did finally come to watch it back those 18 months later, I was surprised how proud of my performance I was. In that round and a half, I gave it my all. When the towel came in and the ref stepped in, I was the one still throwing punches so I proved to myself, as I had against Geale, there was no quit in me.

I had travelled to the lion's den, wanting to take on a great German fighter in his own backyard as much as wanting to earn the money to make my family secure and honour Gary's memory. I fought for all the travelling supporters and the nation as a whole. In my estimation, I went out with my head held high, with all the right motives.

I may not have been able to hear it at the time but a few lines from the lyric of my ring walk music that night, Look Right Through, is my answer to the critics:

I'm quite sure,
That you never knew,
All the pain that I've been through.

29

TONY – 3

"There's probably only one thing Darren and I will look back on and disagree over. He reckoned he over-achieved with the talent he had and the injuries. I can agree with the second part of that but I always knew he had the ability to be a world champion. Had he been fitter for longer, he would have won the title sooner and would have made defences, I'm sure of that.

It's true that Gary was the more naturally gifted but Darren had a work rate that was second to none. He had great determination and a will to win at anything he did – football, swimming, running, anything.

The Geale training camp was probably the best we ever had, but even then he was struggling to get through it and kept breaking down, he was in that much pain. Agony even sometimes. But champions find a way. He drove himself through it, whether he was on a bike or in sparring. He had that ability that you don't see in many fighters. Only champions.

He was always a lovely boxer, too. Right from the start, as well as the grit and determination, he had a lovely jab and very fast hands and feet. I have seen hundreds of kids come in the gym who just didn't have the talent he had.

Inside his head he was a genius. He could work things out. The only way I can put it is that he was like a mathematician who could work out some mad sum put down in front of him. You put someone in the ring with him and he had worked them out within one round. Sometimes in fights he got bored, I think, and got complacent or lost concentration because he was so much on top.

I think God intervened in my life for me to become a boxing trainer. To be the kind of ultimate trainer who takes kids from amateur level to be champion of the world. Not picking them up halfway through their career, but to put everything into them and mould them to make them what they are as boxers and as people.

Physically and mentally he had everything to make it to the top. I knew that straight away and I told him. He might have had those depressions but when he was in the zone in a fight, he was mentally very tough.

He also had that amazing low heart beat, 36 beats a minute resting. You look at a lot of champions in any sport – marathon runners, tennis players – and they have that. It meant that he could keep training when others were tired.

He was worth all the times he threatened to quit, all the troubles. It was like Bryn Robertson said to me once: "We are attracted to things that are broken. That's what the Lord wants." Talented people are often the most self-destructive, aren't they? Paul Gascoigne, Mike Tyson, Ronnie O'Sullivan.

I never wanted him to quit without getting his rewards, both in achievements and financially. That was why I withheld his purse from the Martinez fight for a while, as it came from Eddie through me. I wanted to make sure he bought a house. I told him he wasn't quitting boxing without a house to show for it.

I am really proud of what he and we achieved. I suppose the Sturm fight was the downer and I felt sad at everything about that. It was hard seeing all that, all the build-up and then the night itself. The great shame is that if he had been fit, Darren would have boxed Sturm's head away.

After Gary died, our relationship became more than boxer

and trainer. It became stronger. I look at him like a son. We will stay close, I know that. He will still come to the gym and he will always be welcome. He's part of my family. He's a class act.

Some people ask me how I can be a Christian and yet be in a violent sport. I don't see it as a violent sport, even though people outside of boxing might do. When you become involved, you realise what an art it is. You see the rhythm. It's like a dance. If you are clever, it's like watching art.

There's the cleverness of just evading punches, the cleverness of split second timing, of gliding around the ring, just gliding away from the shots. And there's the cleverness of the timing of getting your punches on target. Because although you are striving for the knockout, you are also striving for the points win. Knockouts come by chance. Points wins come by craft.

I believe that God has a particular role in mind for each and every one of us. I believe that God put Darren Barker on this earth to be a champion and a role model. That's why his story captures people's imagination. He is more interesting than other fighters.”

30

JOGGING WITH A LIMP

The announcement was made formally in mid January of 2014 and it heralded the start of a great year personally, though tinged with a sadness at the death of Gemma's father. Retirement from boxing meant no more starving myself, more time to spend with my family, to be there for and with them - to be present mentally not just physically - rather than being focused on, even obsessed with, a fight. Above all, there were no regrets.

Please don't misinterpret that as ingratitude to the sport of boxing. I had and will always have great respect for the sport, its participants and its fans. It is a great sport and much maligned on occasions. It teaches kids codes of honour and discipline, how to be good people as well as good sporting figures. People talk a lot of nonsense about corruption in it, due to some age-old image, but all I can say is that I never saw any of it, was never offered a bribe or anything like that.

I believe I always conducted myself with dignity and integrity. I tried to be a good ambassador. I boxed with heart and soul, I believe, and gave the paying public value for money. I left everything I had in the ring. And I will always be a world champion, so I accept the need to represent my sport well.

I was not really a born fighter, though. That was Gary. He was the natural in our family. I had some talent, learned good technique and was highly competitive. But it didn't come easy to me and took its toll. When the end came, my mind and body recognised it straight away. And I knew it was time to move on.

It was never really the physical pain that got to me most – the grinding hips and the aching elbows - most of which people never saw as they were endured out of the ring. In fact, there is a lot the fans don't see. After fighting Joe Frazier once, for example, Muhammad Ali said that he was urinating blood for days and I can believe it.

Then there was the stuff people did see in the ring, such as the cuts and bruises, though there were still things that went unnoticed, like head butts and when an opponent would miss with a punch but catch you with an elbow. Some people think as well that gloves are heavily padded and they cushion blows. They don't. They're still hard. Your fists are wrapped with bandages but they can still be human sledgehammers.

Above and beyond the physical issues, it was more the emotional price of boxing to be paid that I could no longer sustain. I put a lot of pressure on myself to deliver, whether that was financial security for my family or winning to keep Gary's memory alive. I always had this overwhelming fear of losing, too. Then there were the black holes of depression half way through training camps, particularly in the early years after Gary died, and being crabby with those around me.

Free from the physical demands and mental strain, I enjoyed my new relaxed life. I appeared on *A Question of Sport* on the BBC. I did a series of articles for *Boxing News* on technical aspects of the sport and I made some appearances on Sky Sports, either on their *Ringside* magazine programme or as a pundit at live fight nights. To be honest, it wasn't always something I really enjoyed as I got so nervous but I was OK if it was a weight that I followed or if the contest involved fighters I knew.

I also did some travelling abroad to comment on fights, to Qatar for Bein Sports, and I retained an interest in the sport. I am a fan of British boxing and want our fighters to do well. I was fortunate to be part of a golden era with men like Carl Froch and Kell Brook around. And I think the sport in Britain is booming with some bright talents coming through, thanks to Eddie Hearn having given it such a lift. That Froch fight against George Groves at Wembley with 80,000 people inside in the summer of 2014 was an amazing promotion.

I also travelled just as a boxing fan. I managed to get tickets from a mate, John Murphy, for the Floyd Mayweather – Manny Pacquiao fight in Las Vegas and I went with Luke Chandler. It was a fantastic occasion, even if the fight was a bit of a damp squib, with Mayweather winning comfortably.

Out there, I ran into Greg Barton, my first opponent when I made my comeback after Gary's death and we chewed the fat. I also got to shake Mike Tyson's hand, though didn't want to remind him about that time in London I annoyed him by sneaking a photo when I was with Gary, Dad and Lee and we were picked to watch him train all those years ago. Then there was an interview with Sky Sports in their media room, which was difficult as Lennox Lewis was behind the camera pulling faces and trying to make me laugh.

Another time I had an emotional encounter with my fellow middleweight Paul Williams, who was now in a wheelchair after being paralysed from the waist down as a result of a motorcycle accident in 2012. "Hi champ," he said to me. It was poignant and touching.

I also travelled to Australia for two weeks, mainly for a holiday but also to make a couple of appearances at boxing gyms. I thought long and hard about it because Gary had won his Junior Commonwealth gold medal out there, and I wanted him to have done something in his short life that I hadn't done.

I talked it over with the family and we agreed that Gary would not have wanted to have felt responsible for stopping me doing something. In the end, I was glad I went and absolutely loved it, going from Melbourne to the beautiful Byron Bay on the East

Coast, then on to sample the sights and delights of Sydney.

Then there was a trek with my old Repton mate Ryan Pickard up Mount Toubkal in the Atlas Mountains in Morocco to raise money for The Play Barn Project, a children's cancer charity. And I signed up with fellow ex-boxers Nicky Piper, Glenn McCrory, Johnny Nelson and Glen Catley to cycle across Cuba to help raise money for the British Boxing Board of Control.

Now and then I went back to see Tony, who moved into a swish new gym near Brentwood. It had carpets and everything and I thought it might make them a bit soft. Not that there was too much soft about Tony's growing stable, that now included the big talent of Kevin Mitchell.

I even helped Tony out myself by doing a bit of training. When he went to Texas with Ricky Burns for a world title fight, taking Kevin and John Ryder out there with him to train them there, Tony asked me to look after those in camp left behind, including O'Hara Davies and Ted Cheeseman.

I was flattered that he trusted me and I enjoyed the three weeks getting back to the gym on a regular basis and going through the rituals of fitness work with the guys, overseeing their regimen, working out their daily training needs.

When he got back, Tony even persuaded me to help him out by sparring with John Ryder, who was, Tony said, in need of a quality opponent in a run-up to a fight. I was really not up for getting back into a ring but I felt I owed John after the time he came out to Canada that time ahead of the Geale fight.

I kept it quiet because I didn't want any arguments with the family, and did four rounds. I hope I helped his development but the aches and pains were beginning to set in by the end. To be honest, there was a part of me that quite enjoyed hitting and being hit again, that felt energised - maybe I was more of a born boxer than I thought - but it was something I was not going to do again. I recognised the onset of trouble again with my hips and elbows.

Afterwards, I had to tell family members what I had done because I had a couple of marks on my face, despite wearing a headguard. Grandad made me swear never to do it again. Gemma wondered why I was putting myself through it all again.

The lowest point of that first year in retirement came when Gemma's Dad Charlie died. He was a smashing guy and he and his wife Janet had been amazing with us in allowing us to live with them while we were waiting for me to earn enough money to get our own house up to standard, then helping us to do it.

Charlie was also very helpful behind the scenes in my boxing career, always supportive, and came to all the fights. When I was struggling financially at times, he would also be generous with his help. He was a sad loss to me as well as leaving a huge hole in Gemma's life.

Against that came the birth of our second child, a boy, in the August and Gem and I did not even need to have a conversation about his name. We just knew who to name him after. Baby Charlie was a strapping young fella and instantly had no choice about becoming a Chelsea fan. Whether he will be a boxer is something I would have serious reservations about, but you have to let kids make their own choices when they are old enough, as I was allowed to.

The funny thing was that my brother Lee's boy George wanted to take up boxing when he turned 12 and we took him over to Repton, where he quickly proved himself a game kid who wanted to learn. It was strange, me trying to impart some of my experience to him and going back over to East London of an evening.

Repton then put him into their annual match against the Dockers of Belfast for his debut in a warm-up bout and we all turned up as a family to cheer him on – even Mum, though she could hardly bear to watch. It was mad, as I was as nervous watching him as I used to be going to watch Gary fight. I never did like that feeling of not being in control like you are when you fight yourself.

George duly won his fight and I recognised the delight in him. That first win is very seductive and leaves you wanting more. I will always remember those words of my Grandad when I started following in Dad's footsteps: "It's starting all over again." It's going to be quite some journey for George, I reckon.

Occasionally people will ask me if I would ever box again, given that I retired at just 32 and Bernard Hopkins was still boxing at the age of 49 – and a world champion at light heavyweight as well.

I did wind my Dad up about fighting again when he phoned me one day just for a chat and asked me where I was and what I was doing. It was April Fool's Day and I thought I would have a laugh with him. I told him I was at Harley Street having a brain scan to get my licence back because I was missing boxing. He was staggered and wondered what the hell I was doing – until I reminded him of the date.

I'm afraid I like my grub too much, enjoy travelling around to watch Chelsea, and love being around Scarlett and Charlie every day, to make a return to the ring. It requires incredible single-mindedness and dedication and it's no good being half-hearted about it. If the hunger's gone, there is no point cheating the public for just another payday. And that spar with John Ryder, though it had elements that excited me again, convinced me that I just couldn't do it any more, either emotionally or physically.

My little spell as Tony's stand-in, training the guys, gave me food for thought, mind. I had thought after the Lee Purdy experience in Atlantic City that it was not for me, but now I was not so sure. The camaraderie of the gym and helping boxers improve has its appeal and I might even take my trainer's licence one day.

As I considered what to do with my the rest of my life long term, I looked into a variety of business ventures – though making sure plenty of my money from the Sturm fight was invested in bricks and mortar - and felt optimistic about the future.

It was all part of a discovery process for me. I wanted time to find the right things for me - boxing or business or even both? The disciplined lifestyle again, or the freedom I initially wanted but which I would have to reconsider? I was certainly busy in retirement, always out and about. I have never been one to sit at home and watch TV all day. Even when I am in charge of the kids, I like to take them out.

I needed time for reflection as I made the transition. I did what I set out to do and more. I would probably even have been happy to have quit after winning my first fight as an amateur and bringing home a trophy that was almost bigger than me to the trophy cabinet Dad had to have made for me and Gary. But like George, that winning feeling keeps drawing you in...

There were the England vests and the Commonwealth Games gold medal, after which everything in my professional career was a bonus. Just to be Southern Area Champion was a big achievement to me. Then becoming the British middleweight champion was something that I was especially proud of.

I look at all the greats that held that title, going back to Randolph Turpin and Terry Downes, Alan Minter and Herol Graham, and I feel honoured to be among them. It is the same with the IBF title, with such men as Marvin Hagler, Roy Jones Junior and Bernard Hopkins listed among the champions. And I am in with them.

I never ducked anybody and I fought the very best in my division, in the shape of Sergio Martinez. And I took the title off a very good fighter in Daniel Geale. I will always have that night and will recall it forever. Every boxer has his night and looks back on it with a lasting pride. That night was mine. Even freaks of nature like Ricky Hatton and Carl Froch who had many great nights will recall one particularly special one.

I suppose I might have been fortunate to operate in that little window between Martinez and Gennady Golovkin dominating the division but there were still plenty of top middleweights operating and my record proves I was one of them.

There was a price to be paid physically, and only relatively late on in my career did I find out I had a hip defect from birth, and it only worsened through my competitive instinct to be the best in training and in the ring. I was, sadly, never going to have longevity as a fighter because of that.

Even now, there is pain in walking too far and I know I will need hip replacement surgery long before I am old. All I can say is that the physical problems represent a price I am happy to have paid for what and who the sport brought me.

I have been lucky with people who came into my life at the right times to help me achieve what I did in my chosen career, from Tony Burns to Tony Sims, Bryn Robertson and Bruce Lloyd, Eddie Hearn and Luke Chandler.

And I have been blessed with people who loved and supported me through the tough times, particularly through Gary's death; Mum and Dad naturally, Nan and Grandad, Lee and Daisy, Uncle Dean, and of course Gemma.

I remember people saying that when it came to Gary and what happened to him, time would be the greatest healer for me. I don't know how that can be because it always hurts so much whenever I think about it. But I do know what Bruce taught me: that it's always going to be a bad wound but it won't always be an open one. It is revealing looking back now, to think that my journey was always about trying to overcome both emotional and physical pain

And I will never forget what Bruce once told me about dealing with it all.

"Darren," he said as he fixed me with his trademark stare and moved his swivel chair closer to mine in his consulting room. "You will probably always walk with a limp. But you will walk." After becoming a world champion, I was almost able to jog with a limp, if not quite run.

I guess that is the message of my story: that adversity and pain can bring out the best in us, force us to reach to the very depths of our being for resilience and resourcefulness, whether that is in the emotional demands of everyday life and the sadnesses and family tragedies that many have to endure, or in the boxing ring where the blows come more literally.

My writer Ian Ridley rang me when we came towards the end of our collaboration asking me for my list of acknowledgements. I thought it over for a week or two before telling him that everyone who has known and helped me is given full credit in the narrative, as they deserve, but there was something to be added.

I want then to end the book with the dedication I gave to Ian for the front of it as I give thanks that while my little brother Gary wasn't around for long and I won't be for ever, my record and my achievements, and the names therefore of Darren and Gary Barker, will be…

For you, Gal. We did it.

DARREN BARKER

PROFESSIONAL RECORD

Won 26 (16 knockouts/technical knockouts)
Lost 2 (2 technical knockouts)

Key: UD – Unanimous decision. TKO – Technical Knockout.
KO – Knockout. RTD – Retired. SD – Split Decision

September 24, 2004 – Ice Arena, Nottingham

Howard Clarke (England)	Won	UD, 6 rounds	1-0

November 12, 2004 – Wembley Conference Centre

David White (England)	Won	TKO, 2nd round	2-0

March 26, 2005 – Hackney Empire

Leigh Wicks (England)	Won	TKO, 4th round	3-0

April 10, 2005 – International Centre, Brentwood

Andrei Sherel (Belarus)	Won	TKO, 3rd round	4-0

July 9, 2005 – Ice Arena, Nottingham

Ernie Smith (England)	Won	UD, 6 rounds	5-0

July 16, 2005 – Prince Regent Hotel, Chigwell, Essex

Dean Walker (England)	Won	UD, 6 rounds	6-0

DARREN BARKER

PROFESSIONAL RECORD

December 2, 2005 – Ice Arena, Nottingham

John Paul Temple (England)	Won	TKO, 6th round	7-0

January 20, 2006 – York Hall, London

Richard Mazurek (England)	Won	UD, 6 rounds	8-0

February 17, 2006 – York Hall, London

Louis Mimoune (France)	Won	TKO, 2nd round	9-0

May 12, 2006 – York Hall, London

Danny Thornton (England)	Won	KO, 6th round	10-0

July 12, 2006 – York Hall, London

Conroy McIntosh (England)	Won	TKO ,7th round	11-0

September 15, 2006 – York Hall, London

Hussain Osman (England)	Won	UD, 10 rounds	12-0

WON SOUTHERN AREA MIDDLEWEIGHT TITLE

November 24, 2006 – Ice Arena, Nottingham

Ojay Abrahams (England)	Won	RTD 1st round	13-0

December 8, 2006 – Goresbrook Centre, Dagenham

Paul Samuels (England)	Won	KO 1st round	14-0

October 5, 2007 – York Hall, London

Greg Barton (England)	Won	TKO, 3rd round	15-0

November 14, 2007 – York Hall, London

Ben Crampton (Australia)	Won	TKO, 7th round	16-0

WON VACANT COMMONWEALTH TITLE

DARREN BARKER

PROFESSIONAL RECORD

February 22, 2008 – York Hall, London

Steven Bendall (England)	Won	TKO, 7th round	17-0

RETAINED COMMONWEALTH TITLE

August 15, 2008 – Enoch, Alberta, Canada

Larry Sharpe (Canada)	Won	UD, 10 rounds	18-0

December 13, 2008 – International Centre, Brentwood

Jason McKay (England)	Won	RTD, 6th round	19-0

RETAINED COMMONWEALTH TITLE

May 23, 2009 – Watford Colosseum

Darren McDermott (England)	Won	TKO, 4th round	20-0

RETAINED COMMONWEALTH TITLE

November 28, 2009 – International Centre, Brentwood

Danny Butler (England)	Won	TKO, 7th round	21-0

WON BRITISH TITLE
RETAINED COMMONWEALTH TITLE

April 9, 2009 – Alexandra Palace, London

Affif Belghecham (France)	Won	UD, 12 rounds	22-0

WON VACANT EUROPEAN TITLE

April 30, 2011 – Olympia, London

Domenico Spada (Italy)	Won	UD, 12 rounds	23-0

WON VACANT EUROPEAN TITLE

October 1, 2011 – Boardwalk Hall, Atlantic City, USA

Sergio Martinez (Argentina)	Lost	TKO, 11th round	23-1

FOR WBC DIAMOND BELT AND THE RING WORLD TITLE

DARREN BARKER
PROFESSIONAL RECORD

December 8, 2012 – Olympia, London

Kerry Hope (Wales)	Won	TKO, 4th round	24-1

March 9, 2013 – Wembley Arena

Simone Rotolo (Italy)	Won	TKO, 4th round	25-1

WON IBF INTERNATIONAL TITLE

August 17, 2014 – Ovation Hall, Atlantic City, USA

Daniel Geale (Australia)	Won	SD, 12 rounds	26-1

WON IBF WORLD TITLE

December 7, 2013 – Porsche Arena, Stuttgart

Felix Sturm (Germany)	Lost	TKO, 2nd round	26-2

LOST IBF WORLD TITLE

PHOTOGRAPHY PLATE SECTION CREDITS

Page 1: Barker family collection.
Page 2: Bottom left: Getty Images. Others: Barker family collection.
Pages 3 and 4: Alex Ridley.
Page 5: Top: Alex Ridley. Others: Barker family collection.
Page 6: Top: Alex Ridley. Bottom: Action Images.
Pages 7, 8, 9, 10, 11, 12, 13 and 14: Alex Ridley.
Page 15: Getty Images.
Page 16: Barker family collection.

BLACK AND WHITE PICTURE CREDITS

Picture of Gary Barker from the Barker family collection.
All others by Alex Ridley.

Books by Ian Ridley

Season In The Cold: A Journey Through English Football

Cantona: The Red and The Black

Tales From the Boot Camps – with Steve Claridge

Addicted – with Tony Adams

Hero and Villain – with Paul Merson

Floodlit Dreams: How to Save a Football Club

Kevin Keegan: An Intimate Portrait of
Football's Last Romantic

Beyond The Boot Camps – with Steve Claridge

There's A Golden Sky:
How 20 Years of the Premier League
Have Changed Football Forever

Added Time: Surviving Cancer, Death Threats
and the Premier League – with Mark Halsey

A Dazzling Darkness:
The Darren Barker Story – with Darren Barker

Also published by Floodlit Dreams

Added Time: Surviving Cancer, Death Threats and the Premier League – Mark Halsey with Ian Ridley

The Boy in Brazil by Seth Burkett

IAN RIDLEY is the author of 11 sports books, including the No. 1 best-selling *Addicted* with former Arsenal and England captain Tony Adams, which was shortlisted for the William Hill Sports Book of the Year award. Three of his other books have also been nominated in the British Sports Book Awards.

Over a 40-year career he has written on sport for *The Guardian*, *The Daily Telegraph*, *The Independent on Sunday*, *The Observer* and *The Mail on Sunday* for whom he was Chief Football Writer. He was named Sports Journalist of the Year in the 2007 British Press Awards and has been nominated on two other occasions.

Once also a scriptwriter with the Sky One drama series *Dream Team*, he remains a contributor to newspapers, radio and television and is also the creator of Floodlit Dreams publishing.